The Mason Jar
DESSERT
COOKBOOK

LONNETTE PARKS

SQUAREONE
PUBLISHERS

COVER DESIGNER: Jeannie Tudor
IN-HOUSE EDITOR: Joanne Abrams
TYPESETTER: Gary A. Rosenberg

Square One Publishers
115 Herricks Road
Garden City Park, NY 11040
(516) 535-2010 • (877) 900-BOOK
www.squareonepublishers.com

Library of Congress Cataloging-in-Publication Data

Parks, Lonnette.
    The Mason jar dessert cookbook : how to create Mason jar
dessert mixes / Lonnette Parks.
        p. cm.
    Includes index.
    ISBN-13: 978-0-7570-0295-3 (pbk.)
    1. Cookies. 2. Cake. 3. Food mixes. I. Title.

TX772.P293   2007
641.8'6—dc22

2006026256

Printed in Canada

10   9   8   7   6   5   4   3   2   1

Contents

Cookies

Brownies and Bar Cookies

Muffins, Scones, and Breads

Cakes and Cupcakes

Jar Cakes

I dedicate this book to my Auntie Eleanor, who treated me as if I were her own daughter. I will forever have fond memories of sitting with her at the kitchen table as she gave me her most treasured Christmas cookie recipes and shared her cooking and baking secrets. She has a special place in my heart and her spirit lives on.

Acknowledgments

A big thank-you to the people at Square One Publishers—Rudy, Joanne, Marie, Bob, and Anthony—for making this book what it is. I am also very grateful to Lesley, my chief kitchen tester, for her invaluable input. Thanks also go to my other kitchen testers, although there are too many to list as I have sent my samples to Madison County High School, Richards Wilbert Inc., and FCC. To my supportive husband, Mike, who has urged me to continue what I've started and not look back, I love you so much. And to my three beautiful children—Kurt, my smart, funny, handsome, and talented musician; Nate, the cutest and most talented baseball player in the USA; and Beth, my beautiful daughter and my friend—I love you all so very much!

Introduction

Everyone loves the aroma of cookies, cakes, and muffins baking in the oven. But with today's busy lifestyles, homemade desserts are for special occasions only—or they were, until Mason jar mixes came along. Decorated with a square of fabric and a brightly colored ribbon, each container holds the nonperishable ingredients—flour, sugar, and the like—needed to create a wonderful dessert. All you have to do is follow the simple instructions on the attached card, and you have a batch of yummy cookies, a pan of fudgy brownies, a warm coffee cake, or an array of tempting scones. No fuss. No bother. Just sweet satisfaction.

If you have ever wanted to create beautiful Mason gift jars in your own home, or try your hand at making the desserts yourself, here's the good news: You don't have to be a craft expert to assemble the containers, nor do you have to be a culinary school graduate to make the recipes in your own kitchen. *The Mason Jar Dessert Cookbook* will show you just how easy it is. Within its pages, you'll find recipes for fifty delectable desserts, including cookies, brownies, muffins, scones, quick breads, cakes, and cupcakes. These sweet treats are easy to make for even the novice baker, and are guaranteed to please family and friends alike.

The book begins with a chapter called "The Basics." The first part of this chapter guides you in buying the best ingredients and equipment for your dessert-making adventures, and provides tips for getting successful results. It then covers all the ins and outs of creating the jars, including what size jar to use; how to make neat, even ingredient layers; and how to add those finishing touches that turn the jar into a beautiful gift.

Following the "Basics" chapter are fifty recipes for heavenly baked treats such as Oatmeal Scotchies, Easy Chocolate Lover's Bars, Banana Snack Cake, Chocolate Chip Cupcakes, and more. Because this book is designed for both the baker *and* the crafter, most recipes have been presented in a two-page spread. Intended for the home baker, the left-hand page contains the recipe itself. Kitchen-tested, each recipe is simple to follow and yields simply scrumptious results. Intended for the crafter, the right-hand page

provides directions for creating the jarred mix. For each dessert, a diagram shows you how to layer the ingredients for attractive results, and a box neatly displays the baking instructions you'll want to include on your gift tag.

For the more adventurous baker, the book also includes recipes for five jar cakes —unique cakes that are actually *baked in Mason jars*. Unique, certainly—but wonderfully simple, too. The easy-to-follow instructions guide you in making a batch of jar cakes in your own kitchen. Then, as the occasion arises, you either present them as ready-to-eat desserts, or you happily eat them yourself. The jar cakes, which vacuum seal as they cool, stay fresh for months in your pantry, waiting to be enjoyed.

So take out your mixing bowl and get ready to experience the joys of Mason jar desserts. Whether you want to fill your kitchen with the aroma of home-baked goods; you'd like to give distinctive Mason jar mixes and cakes to dessert-loving friends and family; or you're searching for a unique fund-raising idea, *The Mason Jar Dessert Cookbook* is all you need. Enjoy the experience!

The**Basics**

Welcome to the world of Mason jar desserts! This book will show you just how easy it is to bake up a variety of delicious desserts—truly scrumptious treats like Butterscotch Brownies, Chocolate Chunk Toffee Cookies, and Blueberry Banana Muffins. It even provides recipes for jar cakes—cakes that are actually *baked in a jar,* where they keep fresh for months until you're ready to enjoy them. Just as important, *The Mason Jar Dessert Cookbook* will guide you in making beautiful Mason jar mixes that will bring the gift of home baking to friends who simply love homemade desserts, but who think they don't have the time to whip them up on their own. (They'll be happy to learn that they're wrong.)

While both Mason jar mixes and the desserts themselves are a snap to make, you'll enjoy the best results if you keep a few guidelines in mind as you select ingredients, create your jar mixes, and turn your mixes into wonderful homemade treats. This chapter provides all the basics, insuring that both your gift jars and your desserts are the best they can be.

INGREDIENTS

All of the ingredients used in the *The Mason Jar Dessert Cookbook* are common, easy-to-find items. While a few of the ingredients, such as dried cherries, are used in only one or two recipes, many, such as flour and sugar, are used in most or all of the recipes in the book. Because these products are so important to the success of your desserts, let's take a few minutes to learn more about them so that you can choose the best ingredients possible for your baked goods.

Flour

Almost all of the recipes in this book call for all-purpose flour, which is a blend of refined hard and soft wheat flours. Choose either bleached or unbleached flour for your desserts, as either one will produce delicious results. The difference is only that the latter type has not undergone a bleaching process, and so contains more vitamin E than its bleached counterpart.

Once opened, flour will stay fresh for up to six months. Simply keep it in a clean, airtight container that prevents the product from absorbing any moisture, and store it in a cool place.

Granulated Sugar

Whenever the word "sugar" is used in this book, the recipe calls for granulated white sugar—although you may also use a super-granulated (superfine) sugar, which is a finer grind that is still coarse enough to have easily discernible crystals. Store your sugar as you would store flour—in a clean, airtight container kept in a cool place.

Brown Sugar

Brown sugar is simply granulated white sugar that has been coated with a film of molasses, and so is more flavorful than its white counterpart. When making your Mason jar desserts, in most cases you can use either light or dark brown sugar—the choice is yours. Just be aware that in addition to being darker in color, dark brown sugar has a more pronounced flavor than light.

Because brown sugar is moister than white sugar, when making cookies, the resulting treats will tend to be delightfully chewy. Be aware, though, that the same moisture which makes brown sugar so irresistible also makes it prone to turn hard and lumpy. To keep your purchase from turning into a rock-hard mass, be sure to store it in an airtight container (doubled zip-lock plastic bags are great) and to keep it in a cool place. If the sugar should become hard, however, simply microwave it, uncovered, for twenty to thirty seconds, or until it becomes soft enough to use with ease.

Eggs

Eggs help provide the structural framework for most of my desserts, allowing them to rise and puff. For best results when making the recipes in this book, use eggs marked "large" and buy the freshest ones you can find. Then refrigerate them and use them before the expiration date.

To keep fat and cholesterol under control, many people now use egg substitutes when cooking and baking. However, egg substitutes will not work well in Mason jar desserts, as the dough they produce is crumbly and dry. For moist and delicious results, always choose the freshest whole eggs when following the recipes in this book.

Butter

For the best flavor and texture, most of my recipes use real sweet (unsalted) butter. If you prefer, you may substitute margarine for the butter, but don't use light butter, light margarine, or diet spreads, as all of these products contain added moisture that will adversely affect the finished desserts. You may also substitute a butter-flavored shortening such as Butter Flavor Crisco. In fact, you'll find that a few of my recipes use shortening—either butter-flavored or plain—instead of butter.

The recipes in this book usually express butter amounts in terms of cups ($\frac{1}{2}$ cup, $\frac{1}{4}$ cup, etc.). These amounts are easy to measure, as one stick of butter ($\frac{1}{4}$ pound) equals $\frac{1}{2}$ cup, or eight tablespoons. Usually, the recipe's ingredients list specifies softened butter. To soften the butter, simply allow it to sit at room temperature for forty-five minutes. Don't leave it out of the refrigerator too long, though, especially when making cookies. Overly soft butter will result in excessive spreading during the baking process. In fact, butter that is too warm *or* too cold can actually alter the temperature of the dough, affecting baking times.

Butter can be stored in either the refrigerator or the freezer. Kept in the refrigerator, butter remains fresh for up to two weeks; in the freezer, for up to six months.

Baking Soda and Baking Powder

The majority of the Mason jar dessert recipes contain one or both of two common forms of leavening—baking soda and baking powder.

Also called bicarbonate of soda and sodium bicarbonate, baking soda is a naturally occurring substance. When used alone, baking soda has no leavening power. However, when used in a batter that also contains an acidic ingredient such as molasses or buttermilk, it causes baked goods to rise.

Baking powder is a mixture of baking soda and other ingredients, the most important of which is an acidic compound such as cream of tartar. When this product is mixed in a batter with wet ingredients, leavening occurs. No acidic ingredients are needed, as the acid is already in the powder.

Why do the recipes in this book sometimes use one of these products and sometimes use both? Clearly, when no acidic ingredient is used in the batter, baking powder is the leavening of choice. However,

other factors also come into play. For instance, baking powder is most appropriate when you're making cookies that are intended to be light colored and puffy. And baking soda can be used to lend a somewhat salty flavor to baked products.

Both baking soda and baking powder are inexpensive and readily available. Stored in covered containers, they will remain fresh and potent for up to six months.

Vanilla Extract

Many of the baked items in this book are flavored with vanilla extract. In preparing your Mason jar dessert recipes, try to use only those products labeled "pure." Imitation extracts are composed of artificial ingredients, and often have a bitter aftertaste. These products can be used, of course, but since a bottle of extract lasts a long time, it makes sense to spend a little more and buy the best.

Oatmeal

In *The Mason Jar Dessert Cookbook*, oatmeal is used in a variety of recipes to add a distinctive yet subtle flavor and a wonderfully chewy texture. When shopping for your

Mason jar mix ingredients, be sure to purchase *instant oatmeal*—oatmeal that cooks up the instant that boiling water is added—as it will produce the best results when making the recipes in this book. This product will stay fresh for up to six months when stored in a clean airtight container.

Nuts

The Mason jar dessert recipes use a variety of nuts—including walnuts, pecans, peanuts, macadamia nuts, and almonds—to add flavor and crunch to baked goods. Feel free to replace one type of nut with another, according to your preferences. But whenever the recipe specifies almonds, it is suggested that you avoid substituting other nuts simply because almonds have such a special and distinctive flavor—one that cannot be replaced by any other nut.

When toasted nuts are called for in a recipe, I simply place the whole nuts (shells removed) in a single layer on an ungreased baking sheet, and pop them into a 275°F oven for about fifteen minutes, or until they are crisp and golden brown. It's important to keep an eye on the nuts as they toast, stirring them occasionally to prevent burning.

Remove the toasted nuts from the oven and allow them to cool before chopping or crushing according to recipe instructions. Nuts must be cooled completely before they are used in a recipe or added to a Mason jar gift mix.

The flavor of nuts is carried by their essential oils, which is the same component that makes all nuts perishable. If you buy nuts in shells, they'll stay fresher, as the shells will protect them from air, moisture, heat, and light. In fact, unshelled nuts can be stored for about twice as long as shelled nuts. If the nuts are already shelled, though, place them in an airtight container and keep the container in a cool, dry, dark place for up to two months before using. To increase the nuts' shelf life, place the container in the refrigerator, where they'll stay fresh for up to four months, or in the freezer, where they can remain for up to six months.

Baking Chips

Chips add color, creaminess, and flavor to desserts. A variety of chips are used in this book, including butterscotch, peanut butter, toffee, milk chocolate, semisweet chocolate, and white chocolate (which contains no chocolate at all). In each of these cases, you will, of course, get the best results when you opt for the highest-quality product available, but this is especially true when selecting any type of chocolate chip. I always use the purest chocolate chips—never chips that are labeled "imitation" chocolate. Although a bit pricier, pure chocolate chips result in a truer chocolate flavor as well as a creamier texture.

If you use only a portion of a bag of chocolate chips, wrap the remaining chips tightly and store in a cool (60°F to 70°F), dry place or in the freezer. If kept in a warm environment, the chocolate may develop pale gray steaks and blotches as the cocoa butter rises to the surface. In damp conditions, chocolate may form tiny gray sugar crystals on the surface. In either case, the chocolate can still be used, but flavor and texture will be slightly affected. Note that because of the milk solids found in milk and white chocolate, these chips should be stored for no longer than nine months. Dark chocolate can remain fresh for up to *ten years* when properly stored. For the very best flavor and texture, though, you'll want to use it within eighteen months.

BASIC KITCHEN EQUIPMENT

Only the simplest of kitchen equipment is needed to bake delicious Mason jar desserts. The following items will make baking an easier, more pleasurable activity, and will help you enjoy success each and every time you select a recipe from this book.

Measuring Cups and Spoons

The accurate measuring of ingredients is essential to baking success whether preparing Mason jar desserts or making any other home-baked treat. And the key to accurate measuring is the proper use of basic measuring cups and spoons.

When measuring dry ingredients such as flour, sugar, and oatmeal, always use dry measuring cups. Available in sets that usually include 1-cup, ½-cup, ⅓-cup, and ¼-cup measures, these cups allow you to spoon or scoop up the ingredient and then level it off with a straight edge—a metal spatula or knife—for greatest accuracy. Never use a liquid measuring cup for this purpose as it will make precise measuring impossible.

When measuring liquid ingredients such as milk, applesauce, or melted butter, be sure to use liquid measuring cups, which are clear cups with markings that indicate 1-, 3/4-, 2/3-, 1/2-, 1/3-, and 1/4-cup levels. For greatest accuracy, place the cup on the counter and bend down to check the amount at eye level.

Always use measuring spoons—not the teaspoons and tablespoons you use to set your table—to measure small amounts of spices and the like. These inexpensive tools come in sets that usually include 1-table-spoon, 1-teaspoon, 1/2-teaspoon, and 1/4-tea-spoon measures. When using dry ingredients, if possible, dip the spoon in the container until it overflows, and then shake the spoon to level it off. When measuring wet ingredients, pour the liquid into the spoon to its maximum capacity.

Mixing Bowls

When preparing the batter or dough for your Mason jar desserts, you'll need just a few different mixing bowls. A small bowl of about 1 quart in size will be called for just occasionally to hold a sugary topping or another single ingredient. More commonly, you'll want a medium-sized bowl (about 2 quarts) and a large bowl (about 3 quarts).

This simple equipment will give you the room you need to blend the butter with the other wet ingredients, mix the dry ingredients, and ultimately combine all of the ingredients together—without making a floury mess on your kitchen counter.

Mixing bowls can be made of a variety of materials, including glass, stainless steel, plastic, and ceramic. If you don't already own a set of bowls, consider buying tempered glass. Glass bowls not only allow you to easily see when the ingredients are well mixed, but also make it possible to microwave ingredients such as chocolate.

Baking Sheets

Every baker has her personal preferences regarding baking sheets. For cookie baking, I feel that I get the best results with air cushion sheets, which are made of two layers of metal with a "layer" of air in between. The dual layered sheets allow air to better circulate under the cookie-baking surface, reducing hot spots so that cookies bake beautifully all across the sheet, and not just in the middle. These sheets come with both nonstick and regular surfaces. Either surface will yield great results.

To insure even baking, use a cookie sheet that fits in the oven with at least one inch to spare around each edge. Whether or not your sheet is nonstick, it is not necessary to grease the baking surface unless it is called for in the recipe. When greasing is recommended, either coat the pan lightly with cooking spray or rub a small amount of butter or shortening evenly over the pan.

Baking Pans

Baking pans come in all sorts of shapes and sizes. Over the years, I have accumulated quite a variety; however, I find that I get the most mileage out of just a few. The cake and bar cookie recipes in this book require an 8-inch square, 9-inch square, or 9-x-13-inch rectangular pan. Bundt cakes need a 9-inch (9 cup) bundt pan, and the breads are baked in 9-x-5-inch loaf pans. For the muffins and cupcakes, a standard tin for making 3-inch muffins is required.

Baking pans come with both nonstick and regular surfaces. Whether or not your pans are nonstick, it is not necessary to grease the baking surface unless it is called for in the recipe. As with the cookie sheets, when greasing is recommended, either coat the pan lightly with cooking spray or rub a small amount of butter or shortening evenly over its bottom and sides.

Electric Mixers

While an electric mixer is by no means a baking necessity, if you do have one on hand, it will make quick work of mixing together creamy ingredients such as softened butter with eggs and sugar, and in some cases can be used to combine the wet ingredients with the dry. Either a portable (hand-held) or a stationary (stand) mixer can be used—although I personally like a portable model. If you don't have a mixer, wet ingredients can usually be blended with a whisk or fork, and wet and dry ingredients can be combined with a sturdy wooden spoon and a little hard work. Your desserts will be just as delicious.

Baking Racks

Most of the recipes in this book direct you to first cool the dessert on the pan for several minutes, and then transfer it to a baking rack for further cooling. Made of wire, these racks speed the cooling process by allowing air to flow around both the tops and bottoms of cookies, muffins, or other treats. In most cases, your Mason jar creations will be ready for serving or storage within twenty minutes.

If you don't own cooling racks, you can simply transfer the desserts directly from the baking sheet to a plate or a long sheet of waxed paper. Be aware, though, that the moisture from the hot baked goods may make them slightly adhere to the plate or waxed paper. Once the desserts have cooled, be sure to lift items such as cookies carefully to avoiding breakage.

BAKING TIPS

The recipes in this book are easy to follow for even the beginning baker. Just keep a few simple guidelines in mind, and you're sure to bake mouth-watering desserts each and every time you select a Mason jar recipe.

Measuring the Ingredients

Earlier in the chapter, I mentioned the importance of accurately measuring each ingredient. (See page 8.) In addition to following the fundamental guidelines presented in that discussion, keep these tips in mind when preparing your various Mason jar doughs and batters.

❏ There's no need to sift the flour before—or after—measuring it for your Mason jar desserts. However, keep in mind that the amount of flour used is crucial, so care should be taken to avoid adding more flour than recommended. To keep the flour light and the measurement true, either dip the cup in the flour bin or spoon the flour into the cup before leveling with a straight edge, such as a spatula or knife.

❏ When measuring molasses, peanut butter, honey, or any other sticky ingredient, grease the cup first to facilitate easy removal. A rubber spatula will further aid you in scraping every last bit out of the cup.

❏ When measuring butter, soften the butter only until it is malleable enough to be packed into a dry measuring cup. Then level off the top with a straight edge.

❏ Measure all brown sugar by packing it firmly into a dry measuring cup and leveling it off with a straight edge. When the sugar is turned out of the cup, it should hold its shape.

❏ When measuring raisins and other soft, chunky ingredients, press them into the measuring cup. When measuring dry, chunky ingredients—chocolate chips and chopped nuts, for instance—spoon the ingredient into the cup, tap the cup against the table to make the ingredients settle, and add more if necessary.

Mixing the Batter or Dough

Nearly every Mason jar dessert recipe requires that before mixing the dry ingredients with the wet, you blend the butter or other shortening with one or more of the other wet ingredients, such as the vanilla extract or the egg. This is an important step as it helps insure the proper blending of the batter or dough ingredients. It also incorporates air into the batter, which will enable your baking soda and baking powder to do their work. Although I use a portable mixer to blend the required wet ingredients, this step can also be performed with a whisk or a fork. Just keep mixing

or beating until the ingredients are well blended and the mixture is light in color and fluffy.

Once the butter mixture has been blended, most recipes will direct you to add the dry ingredients to the butter. In some cases, the ingredients can be combined with either a wooden spoon or an electric mixer set on low speed. Be aware, though, that when the dry ingredients include chocolate chips or other goodies that might be chopped up by an electric mixer, it's best to use a spoon. Whichever tool you use, do not overmix the batter, but follow the recipe's directions exactly, mixing either until the ingredients are well combined or for the amount of time specified in the recipe.

Forming and Baking Cookies

The vast majority of Mason jar cookies are drop cookies, meaning that you form the cookies by scooping the dough up with a teaspoon and dropping it onto the baking sheet. Cookie doughs vary in consistency. Some will fall easily from the spoon, and some may need a push from a second spoon. To make the cookies uniform in size, use a measuring teaspoon rather than the teaspoon from your everyday flatware, and scoop up a heaping spoonful.

When a recipe directs you to form the dough into balls, make sure that the dough is stiff enough to handle easily. If not, chill the dough until it reaches the proper consistency and, if necessary, lightly dust your hands with a little flour or powdered sugar to prevent the dough from sticking. With a little practice, you'll soon be able to form balls of a consistent size.

As the cookies are formed, place them at least two inches apart on your cookie sheet to allow for spreading. It is not necessary to grease the baking sheet unless the recipe specifically directs you to do so. Bake only one cookie sheet at a time, and make sure the sheet is on the middle rack of the oven with at least one inch between the edge of the pan and the oven itself. This will promote proper air flow and even heating.

Checking for Doneness of Baked Goods

In most cases, cookies are done when they are slightly browned around the edges. Since baking time and oven temperature affect the cookie's final texture, you may choose to make adjustments according to your personal preferences. If you want your cookies to be chewy, slightly underbake them. If you want them to be crisp, bake them a little longer. Just use a watchful eye when baking cookies, as they can quickly turn from *done* to *hard*. When your cookies are ready to be removed from the oven, place the baking sheet on a heatproof surface for one to five minutes, as specified in the recipe, to allow the cookies to cool slightly. Then use a spatula to transfer the cookies to a rack or plate, and cool the cookies completely before serving or storing them in a container.

Most cakes, cupcakes, muffins, and breads are finished baking when a toothpick inserted in their center comes out dry. Like cookies, these desserts should be allowed to sit for five to ten minutes before they are removed from their pans. If released too soon, a cake may crack or crumble apart.

Keep in mind that most ovens run either a little hotter or a little cooler than the temperature to which they're set, so be aware that you may have to compensate by adjusting either the temperature to which the oven is set or the baking time. (If desired, use an oven thermometer to determine the precise temperature.)

JAR CAKES

The Mason Jar Dessert Cookbook includes a special section of recipes for jar cakes— cakes that are actually baked in Mason jars. Jar cakes are easy to make and fun to give as gifts. You bake the cakes in your own oven, decorate the jars just as you would a Mason jar mix, and then give them—ready to eat— to friends and family. When properly baked and sealed, the cakes will literally stay fresh for *months.* Then, when the recipient wants a dessert big enough for two, she can open the jar, slide the cake out, and enjoy.

Typically, just about any homemade cake recipe will work, but you'll want to avoid commercial (boxed) cake mixes, as they tend to produce poor results. Of course, the recipes that appear on pages 122 to 131 were made especially for jar baking and produce spectacular results. Each recipe will produce several cakes, so you'll be able to give some as gifts *and* keep some for yourself.

As already mentioned, jar cakes are simple to make. But in order to get good results

—and especially the good seal that gives jar cakes such a long shelf life—you do have to understand and follow a few guidelines. Below, you'll learn about the proper way to prepare these unique gifts.

Making Jar Cakes

All of my jar cakes are baked in wide-mouth pint-size jars. Some recipes use six jars, and some use eight. Your first step is to thoroughly clean and dry the number of pint-size jars required for the recipe, and spray the interior of each jar with nonstick cooking spray. Then prepare your batter as directed in the recipe and place a level cup of batter in each of the jars, filling it half full. Using a clean paper towel, wipe any batter from the lip of the lid.

Arrange the jars, uncovered, on a baking sheet, and bake them for the recommended amount of time. You'll know the cakes are done when a toothpick inserted in the center comes out clean.

As soon as the jars are removed from the oven, tightly secure the lid and screw the band onto each hot jar. *Be sure to use potholders to screw the lids on, as the jars will be hot!*

Then transfer the jars to a heatproof surface and allow them to cool completely.

As the jars cool, you will hear a "ping" sound, indicating that a vacuum has formed and the seal is complete. Wait twelve to twenty-four hours after baking, and test the seals as directed below. You will then be able to decorate the jars according to the instructions on page 21.

Testing Jar Cake Seals

Even if your jars made the distinctive "ping" sound when cooling, you'll want to make sure that each and every one is properly sealed. This is important because while a sealed jar cake will keep fresh for months, the cake in an improperly sealed jar will have to be refrigerated and eaten within a few days.

First, wait until the jars have cooled for twelve to twenty-four hours. Then test the seals using one of the following techniques.

❏ **Test 1.** Press the middle of the lid with a finger or thumb. If the lid springs up when you release your finger, the jar is not properly sealed. The lid of a well-sealed jar will have no give.

❏ **Test 2.** Tap the lid with the bottom of a teaspoon. If it makes a dull sound, the lid is not sealed. If the jar is sealed correctly, it will make a distinctive high-pitched ringing sound.

❏ **Test 3.** Hold the jar at eye level and look across the lid. The lid should be concave (curved down slightly in the center). If the center of the lid is either flat or bulging, it may not be sealed.

If you find that any jars have not been properly sealed, you'll want to refrigerate them and eat the cake within a couple of days. Jars with proper seals, however, will keep fresh for four months. Just label and date the jars, and store them in a cool, dark, dry place. For best quality, store between 50 and 70°F.

Usually, jar cakes stay fresh for the full four months, and emerge from their containers moist and delicious. But like all home-preserved foods, these cakes should be examined for signs of spoilage before you either give them as gifts or eat them yourself. The growth of dangerous bacteria and yeast produces gas, which swells the lids and breaks the vacuum seals. So as each stored jar is selected for use, you'll want to examine its lid for tightness. Lids with concave centers have good seals. When you remove the lid, look for cotton-like mold—which can be white, blue, black, or green in color—on the food itself or on the underside of the lid. It should go without saying that a cake which shows any sign of spoilage should be immediately discarded without being tasted.

Be aware that although the Mason jars themselves, as well as the screw band part of the lid, can be reused time and time again, the flat lids cannot. Each flat lid has a sealing compound around the edge, and this compound works only once. Every time you make jar cakes, therefore, you'll want to use new flat lids. You'll also want to make sure that the screw bands are free of rust and without dents or bends. The bands, the lids, and the rims of the jars themselves have to be in perfect shape to produce a solid seal.

Finally, always keep in mind that although jar cakes, when properly made, are both delicious and safe to eat, they require a little more attention to detail than the Mason jar dessert mixes. For that reason, you'll want to carefully follow each of the steps outlined above, including the testing of the seal; be alert to signs of spoilage; and make sure that the desserts are eaten within four months of baking.

Enjoying Jar Cakes

When people first hear about jar cakes, they often wonder how the cake is removed from the jar. After all, even a wide-mouth Mason jar narrows a little at the top, so it certainly seems that the cake would get stuck. The fact is that as the cake bakes and cools, it shrinks slightly from the sides of the jar, making it narrow enough to fit through the Mason jar mouth. To enjoy your cake, you need only run a butter knife around the jar to loosen the cake and then tip the jar, allowing the dessert to slide out.

CREATING THE GIFT JARS

Although you'll want to bake and enjoy Mason jar desserts often, you'll also take pleasure in giving Mason jar dessert mixes and jar cakes to friends and family. Both the jar cakes and the mixes make perfect gifts during the holidays, on birthdays, or just as thoughtful thank-yous.

Fortunately, these gift jars are easy and fun to create. Below, you'll learn about the few simple materials you'll need to get started, and you'll discover how to use them to craft beautiful presents that are a joy to give and receive.

Choosing the Materials

The materials needed to make Mason jar dessert mixes and jar cakes are inexpensive and few in number. Keep these items on hand, and you'll be able to create a gift at a moment's notice.

The Jar

For each dessert mix you make, you will need a clean, dry Mason jar—a wide-mouth jar with a screw-on top—in either a quart or pint size, depending on the recipe. While other containers may also be suitable, the large opening of a Mason jar will give you the room you need to pour in the ingredients; tamp them down into even layers when necessary; and periodically wipe the inside of the jar with a dry paper towel dur-

ing filling so that the final gift has a neat, clean appearance.

For each jar cake, you will need a wide-mouth one-pint Mason jar with a new (unused) flat lid. (For more information on this, see page 16.)

The Fabric and Tie

When you finish creating your Mason jar mix, the appealing layers of ingredients—brown sugar, raisins, and chocolate chips, for instance—will instantly turn the container into an attractive gift. And, of course, the moist jar cakes have their own charm. Many people, in fact, use the unadorned jars to decorate their kitchens and pantries! However, you can further enhance the appeal of the gift by tying a square of decorative fabric to the top.

For each quart-size jar, you will need a seven-by-seven-inch piece of fabric, cut with either regular fabric scissors or pinking shears. Pint-size jars require a six-by-six-inch square. When choosing your fabric, be creative. A square of denim, burlap, or calico would create a delightful country look, for instance, while a red-and-green fabric would be the perfect finishing touch for a Christmas gift. Often, fabric stores offer inexpensive remnants, each of which could adorn several jars.

Be sure to select a tie that complements your fabric. A length of sisal twine or yarn would make an appropriate tie for your calico square, for example, while a slender gold or silver ribbon would beautifully complete your holiday gift. Just make sure that the tie is long enough. A forty-eight-inch length will allow you to securely attach the fabric, as well as your tag, to the jar.

The Tag

When making dessert mix gifts, your tag will provide the all-important information that the recipient of the jar will need to turn the mix into a homemade treat. Each tag should supply the name of the dessert, the yield of the recipe, the list of ingredients that must be added to the mix (eggs and butter, for instance), and the baking instructions themselves. When making jar cake gifts, each tag should supply the name of the cake; should explain how to remove the cake from the jar; and, for safety, should direct the recipient to serve the dessert within a week's time.

Feel free to make a no-fuss tag or to craft one that showcases your creativity and flair. Each recipe contains a boxed copy of the information that belongs on its tag. If you like, you can simply make a photocopy of this box, using the paper of your choice; cut the photocopy out with plain scissors or pinking shears; and attach the printed tag to your jar with the selected tie. Or you may choose to cut out a piece of sturdy paper—a three-by-four-inch size is usually adequate for the dessert mixes—and write out the information in your own clear handwriting or in calligraphy. If you have a computer, of course, your options are even greater. Consider typing in the information and printing it out in a beautiful (but readable) font. Add a decorative border, if you wish. You can even print the information directly onto stickers and affix a sticker to each jar in place of a tag. The possibilities are endless.

Packing the Dessert Mix Ingredients

Most of the recipes in this book include ingredients that can be attractively layered in the Mason jars. Believe it or not, the order in which the ingredients are packed in your Mason jar can make a *big* difference. Imagine, for instance, pouring the granulated sugar over a layer of chocolate chips. Gradually, the sugar would sift between the chips, mixing the layers and creating a messy appearance. That's why the white sugar is so often placed below any chips, dried fruits, or nuts, or over a layer of brown sugar or oatmeal.

By following the order prescribed on the right-hand page of each two-page recipe spread, you will be sure to create an attractive jar. Be aware, though, that in most cases, this isn't the *only* way in which the ingredients can be successfully layered. I have usually chosen to provide you with the simplest method of packing the jar. If you prefer, you can break some of the ingredients into two parts and create your own custom jar of contrasting layers. To keep your layers as neat as possible, just remember to avoid placing powdery or granular ingredients—flour and sugar, for instance—above a product such as chocolate chips, nuts, or raisins. Because chips and the like have space between the individual pieces, they will allow the powdery substance to sift in. Instead, try to pack these goodies at the top of the jar, or place an ingredient such as brown sugar above them, as the moist sugar will form a "seal," preventing the layers from blending together.

When placing ingredients in the Mason jar—especially flour, cocoa, and other powdery ingredients—you might find a wide-mouth canning funnel to be a helpful tool. Placed over the top of the jar, this functional piece of equipment helps guide the ingredients into the jar easily and neatly. Made of plastic or stainless steel, canning funnels are found in most stores that sell kitchen tools and gadgets. You can also purchase funnels online at sites such as www.cooking.com and www.DoItBest. com. Finally, it is easy to make your own canning funnel. Just follow the simple steps presented on page 20.

When creating most Mason jar mix gifts, you will have to pack the ingredients firmly. After pouring in each ingredient, use a long-handled tart tamper; the squeezable bulb section of a turkey baster; or the bottom of a long, slim glass to press the addition into an even layer. Then, before adding the next ingredient, wipe the inside of the jar with a dry paper towel to achieve a clean, professional appearance. Just be sure to follow the

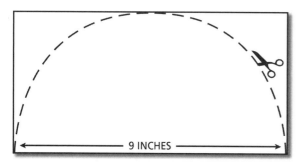

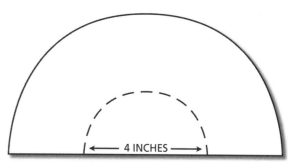

1. Cut a 9-inch semi-circle out of oak tag or other stiff paper.

2. Cut a 4-inch semi-circle from the center of the paper, as shown above.

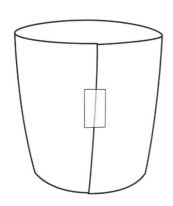

3. Bring the two sides together and attach with tape.

Making a Wide-Mouth Funnel

directions on the right-hand page of each recipe, as some mixes should not be firmly pressed into the jar, but will better fill the jar if added in loose layers.

After all the layers of the dessert mix have been added, simply screw on the top of the jar, tightening it as much as possible to keep the mix fresh. Now you're ready to complete the gift.

Decorating the Jar

To add the finishing touches to your gift mix or jar cake, simply center the chosen fabric square on the lid of the jar and secure it with a rubber band. Then wrap your chosen tie around the rubber band twice, covering the band, and knot the tie to hold it in place.

Using a hole punch, make a hole in the tag and slide the tie through the hole, threading it through once or twice and tying it off with a bow. If you've chosen to photocopy the boxed tag provided on the right-hand page of each recipe, you may want to fold the left side of the tag over the right before punching a hole in the top left-hand corner. This will allow you to thread the tie through two layers of paper, attaching your tag securely to the jar.

Finally, to make your Mason jar gift even more special, you may want to use the same ribbon or twine to attach a wooden spoon or other baking essential to the jar. Your Mason jar gift is now done, ready for its lucky recipient!

HOW TO USE THIS BOOK

The Mason Jar Dessert Cookbook has a truly unique format that allows you to easily bake desserts in your kitchen or create a beautiful Mason jar dessert mix or jar cake gift.

First, use the table of contents or the index to choose a recipe that suits your fancy. For all the recipes except the jar cakes, you will discover that the directions fall on two facing pages. On the left-hand page, you'll find complete instructions for baking the dessert at home. On the right-hand page, you'll find instructions for creating a Mason jar dessert mix.

If you have decided to bake a dessert, simply look at the left-hand page of the two-page recipe spread. You'll see that the ingredients have been broken into two lists. The first list—the Jar Ingredients—contains the nonperishable ingredients that would be placed in the jar if you were creating a mix. These items have been grouped together here for ease of mixing, as in most cases, all the Jar Ingredients are combined first. The second list presents the Additional Ingredients—the eggs, butter, and other items that must be added to the mix to create the dessert. The numbered instructions tell you exactly how to use your ingredients to bake a delicious dessert each and every time.

If your goal is to craft a dessert mix gift, look at the right-hand page. The numbered material at the top of the page outlines the steps for creating the jar. (For more details, see pages 16 to 21 of this chapter.) Next to these instructions, you'll find a diagram that shows you how to fill the jar for attractive results. (Just remember that the ingredients

layer shown at the *bottom* of the diagram should be placed in the jar *first*.) Finally, at the bottom of the page, you'll find all the information you need for your tag. As discussed on page 18, you can photocopy the tag directly from the book and attach the copy to your jar, or, if you prefer, you can write these instructions out on decorative paper.

Baking is a wonderfully satisfying experience. With very little fuss or bother, you can produce delightful confections that are sure to bring smiles to the faces of friends and family alike. In addition, with *The Mason Jar Dessert Cookbook,* you can also give the gift of home baking to everyone on your gift list. However you choose to use this book, I'm sure it will bring pleasing results and a satisfied sweet tooth. Enjoy!

Cookies

BANANANUTCOOKIES

YIELD:
3 DOZEN COOKIES

QUART-SIZE JAR INGREDIENTS

1 1/2 cups all-purpose flour

1 1/2 cups instant oatmeal

1 cup sugar

1/2 cup finely chopped walnuts

1 teaspoon cinnamon

1 teaspoon baking powder

1/2 teaspoon salt

1/4 teaspoon nutmeg

1/4 teaspoon baking soda

ADDITIONAL INGREDIENTS

1 cup mashed ripe banana

1/2 cup butter, softened

2 eggs

1/2 teaspoon vanilla extract

This not-too-sweet cookie is moist and cakelike, with an aroma that will remind you of your favorite banana bread.

1. Preheat the oven to 375°F.

2. Place all of the jar ingredients in a medium-sized bowl, and stir until well combined. Set aside.

3. Place the banana, butter, eggs, and vanilla extract in a large bowl, and blend with a whisk, a fork, or an electric mixer set on low speed.

4. Add the dry ingredients to the banana mixture, and stir with a wooden spoon until well combined.

5. Drop the dough by heaping teaspoonfuls onto an ungreased baking sheet, spacing the cookies about 2 inches apart to allow for spreading.

6. Bake for 10 to 12 minutes, or until the edges are light brown in color. Cool for 1 minute on the baking sheet. Then transfer to wire racks and cool completely.

7. Serve immediately, or store in an airtight container for up to 10 days.

CREATING THE JAR

½ cup finely chopped walnuts

1 ½ cups instant oatmeal

¼ teaspoon nutmeg

1 teaspoon cinnamon

1 cup sugar

½ teaspoon salt

¼ teaspoon baking soda

1 teaspoon baking powder

1 ½ cups all-purpose flour

1. Wash and thoroughly dry a 1-quart wide-mouth canning jar.

2. Layer the ingredients in the jar as shown at left, pressing firmly with a flat-bottomed object, such as a tart tamper or the bottom of a narrow glass, after each addition. Make the layers as level as possible.

3. Secure the lid, and decorate as desired. (See page 21.) Attach the instructions for making the cookies found below.

Yield:
3 dozen cookies

In addition to the contents of the jar, you will need to add the following ingredients:

1 cup mashed ripe banana

½ cup butter, softened

2 eggs

½ teaspoon vanilla extract

BANANA NUT COOKIES

Preheat the oven to 375°F. In a large bowl, blend the banana, butter, eggs, and vanilla extract. Add the contents of the jar, and stir until well mixed. Drop the dough by heaping teaspoonfuls onto an ungreased baking sheet, spacing the cookies about 2 inches apart. Bake for 10 to 12 minutes, or until the edges are light brown in color. Allow to cool for 1 minute on the baking sheet. Then transfer to wire racks and cool completely. Serve immediately, or store in an airtight container for up to 10 days.

BUTTERMILKRAISIN COOKIES

YIELD:
3 DOZEN COOKIES

QUART-SIZE JAR INGREDIENTS

2 cups all-purpose flour

I cup brown sugar, packed

I cup dark raisins

$^1/_2$ cup chopped walnuts

$^1/_2$ teaspoon baking soda

$^1/_2$ teaspoon baking powder

$^1/_4$ teaspoon salt

ADDITIONAL INGREDIENTS

$^3/_4$ cup buttermilk

$^1/_2$ cup butter, softened

I egg

When my husband, Mike, was a young boy, his Aunt Edna used to serve these gems at family gatherings. Because I was fortunate enough to inherit the recipe, Mike is still able to enjoy this childhood favorite today.

1. Preheat the oven to 375°F.

2. Place all of the jar ingredients in a medium-sized bowl, and stir until well combined. Set aside.

3. Place the buttermilk, butter, and egg in a large bowl, and blend with a whisk, a fork, or an electric mixer set on low speed.

4. Add the dry ingredients to the buttermilk mixture, and stir with a wooden spoon until well combined.

5. Drop the dough by heaping teaspoonfuls onto an ungreased baking sheet, spacing the cookies about 2 inches apart to allow for spreading.

6. Bake for 10 to 12 minutes, or until the edges are light brown in color. Allow to cool for 1 minute on the baking sheet. Then transfer to wire racks and cool completely.

7. Serve immediately, or store in an airtight container for up to 1 week.

CREATINGTHEJAR

½ cup chopped walnuts

I cup dark raisins

I cup brown sugar, packed

¼ teaspoon salt

½ teaspoon baking powder

½ teaspoon baking soda

2 cups all-purpose flour

1. Wash and thoroughly dry a 1-quart wide-mouth canning jar.

2. Layer the ingredients in the jar as shown at left, pressing firmly with a flat-bottomed object, such as a tart tamper or the bottom of a narrow glass, after each addition. Make the layers as level as possible.

3. Secure the lid, and decorate as desired. (See page 21.) Attach the instructions for making the cookies found below.

Yield:
3 dozen cookies

In addition to the contents of the jar, you will need to add the following ingredients:

¾ cup buttermilk

½ cup butter, softened

I egg

Buttermilk Raisin Cookies

Preheat the oven to 375°F. In a large bowl, blend the buttermilk, butter, and egg. Add the contents of the jar, and stir until well mixed. Drop the dough by heaping tea-spoonfuls onto an ungreased baking sheet, spacing the cookies about 2 inches apart. Bake for 10 to 12 minutes, or until the edges are light brown in color. Allow to cool for 1 minute on the baking sheet. Then transfer to wire racks and cool completely. Serve immediately, or store in an airtight container for up to 1 week.

BUTTERSCOTCHCHEWIES

*Butterscotch lovers are sure to fall in love with
this soft and temptingly sweet cookie.*

YIELD:
4 DOZEN COOKIES

**QUART-SIZE JAR
INGREDIENTS**

2 cups all-purpose
flour

1 1/4 cups
butterscotch-flavored
chips

1 cup light brown
sugar, packed

1 teaspoon cinnamon

1 teaspoon
baking powder

1/2 teaspoon
baking soda

1/2 teaspoon salt

**ADDITIONAL
INGREDIENTS**

2/3 cup solid butter-
flavored shortening,
such as Butter Flavor
Crisco

2 eggs

1 teaspoon
vanilla extract

1. Preheat the oven to 400°F.

2. Place all of the jar ingredients in a medium-sized bowl, and stir until well combined. Set aside.

3. Place the shortening, eggs, and vanilla extract in a large bowl, and blend with a whisk, a fork, or an electric mixer set on low speed.

4. Add the dry ingredients to the shortening mixture, and stir with a wooden spoon until well combined.

5. Drop the dough by heaping teaspoonfuls onto an ungreased baking sheet, spacing the cookies about 2 inches apart to allow for spreading.

6. Bake for 7 to 9 minutes, or until the edges are light brown in color. Allow to cool for 2 minutes on the baking sheet. Then transfer to wire racks and cool completely.

7. Serve immediately, or store in an airtight container for up to 1 week.

CREATINGTHEJAR

1¼ cups butterscotch-flavored chips

1 cup light brown sugar, packed

1 teaspoon baking powder

½ teaspoon baking soda

½ teaspoon salt

1 teaspoon cinnamon

2 cups all-purpose flour

1. Wash and thoroughly dry a 1-quart wide-mouth canning jar.

2. Layer the ingredients in the jar as shown at left, pressing firmly with a flat-bottomed object, such as a tart tamper or the bottom of a narrow glass, after each addition. Make the layers as level as possible.

3. Secure the lid, and decorate as desired. (See page 21.) Attach the instructions for making the cookies found below.

Yield:
4 dozen cookies

In addition to the contents of the jar, you will need to add the following ingredients:

⅔ cup solid butter-flavored shortening, such as Butter Flavor Crisco

2 eggs

1 teaspoon vanilla extract

BUTTERSCOTCH CHEWIES

Preheat the oven to 400°F. In a large bowl, blend the shortening, eggs, and vanilla extract. Add the contents of the jar, and stir until well mixed. Drop the dough by heaping teaspoonfuls onto an ungreased baking sheet, spacing the cookies about 2 inches apart. Bake for 7 to 9 minutes, or until the edges are light brown in color. Allow to cool for 2 minutes on the baking sheet. Then transfer to wire racks and cool completely. Serve immediately, or store in an airtight container for up to 1 week.

CHERRYJELL-OCOOKIES

*Who would have thought that a favorite childhood dessert
could be transformed into a wonderful cookie?*

**YIELD:
3 DOZEN COOKIES**

**QUART-SIZE JAR
INGREDIENTS**

2 1/2 cups all-purpose
flour

1/2 cup sugar

One (3-ounce)
package cherry Jell-O
gelatin

1 teaspoon
baking powder

1 teaspoon salt

**ADDITIONAL
INGREDIENTS**

3/4 cup butter,
softened

2 eggs

1 teaspoon
vanilla extract

1. Preheat the oven to 375°F.

2. Place all of the jar ingredients in a medium-sized bowl, and stir until well combined. Set aside.

3. Place the butter, eggs, and vanilla extract in a large bowl, and blend with a whisk, a fork, or an electric mixer set on low speed.

4. Add the dry ingredients to the butter mixture, and stir with a wooden spoon until well combined.

5. Drop the dough by heaping teaspoonfuls onto an ungreased baking sheet, spacing the cookies about 2 inches apart to allow for spreading.

6. Bake for 10 to 12 minutes, or until the edges are light brown in color. Allow to cool for 5 minutes on the baking sheet. Then transfer to wire racks and cool completely.

7. Serve immediately, or store in an airtight container for up to 2 weeks.

CREATING THE JAR

1. Wash and thoroughly dry a 1-quart wide-mouth canning jar.

2. Loosely layer the ingredients in the jar as shown at left, making each layer as level as possible without pressing it down.

3. Secure the lid, and decorate as desired. (See page 21.) Attach the instructions for making the cookies found below.

½ cup sugar

One (3-ounce) package cherry Jell-O gelatin

1 teaspoon baking powder

1 teaspoon salt

2½ cups all-purpose flour

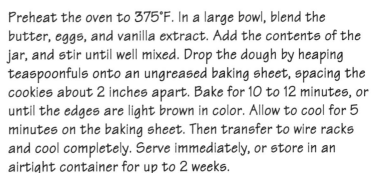

Yield:
3 dozen cookies

In addition to the contents of the jar, you will need to add the following ingredients:

¾ cup butter, softened

2 eggs

1 teaspoon vanilla extract

CHERRY JELL-O COOKIES

Preheat the oven to 375°F. In a large bowl, blend the butter, eggs, and vanilla extract. Add the contents of the jar, and stir until well mixed. Drop the dough by heaping teaspoonfuls onto an ungreased baking sheet, spacing the cookies about 2 inches apart. Bake for 10 to 12 minutes, or until the edges are light brown in color. Allow to cool for 5 minutes on the baking sheet. Then transfer to wire racks and cool completely. Serve immediately, or store in an airtight container for up to 2 weeks.

CHOCOLATECHUNK TOFFEECOOKIES

YIELD:
3 DOZEN COOKIES

QUART-SIZE JAR INGREDIENTS

1 ¼ cups all-purpose flour

1 cup chopped chocolate-covered toffee, such as Heath toffee bar

¾ cup brown sugar, packed

¾ cup semisweet chocolate chips

½ teaspoon baking soda

¼ teaspoon salt

ADDITIONAL INGREDIENTS

½ cup butter, softened

1 egg

1 teaspoon vanilla extract

This yummy twist on the traditional chocolate chip cookie adds bits of chocolate-covered toffee to the mix.

1. Preheat the oven to 375°F.

2. Place all of the jar ingredients in a medium-sized bowl, and stir until well combined. Set aside.

3. Place the butter, egg, and vanilla extract in a large bowl, and blend with a whisk, a fork, or an electric mixer set on low speed.

4. Add the dry ingredients to the butter mixture, and stir with a wooden spoon until well combined.

5. Drop the dough by heaping teaspoonfuls onto an ungreased baking sheet, spacing the cookies about 2 inches apart to allow for spreading.

6. Bake for 10 to 12 minutes, or until the edges are light brown in color. Allow to cool for 2 minutes on the baking sheet. Then transfer to wire racks and cool completely.

7. Serve immediately, or store in an airtight container for up to 1 week.

CREATING THE JAR

I cup chopped chocolate-covered toffee, such as Heath toffee bar

¾ cup brown sugar, packed

¾ cup semisweet chocolate chips

½ teaspoon baking soda

¼ teaspoon salt

I ¼ cups all-purpose flour

1. Wash and thoroughly dry a 1-quart wide-mouth canning jar.

2. Layer the ingredients in the jar as shown at left, pressing firmly with a flat-bottomed object, such as a tart tamper or the bottom of a narrow glass, after each addition. Make the layers as level as possible.

3. Secure the lid, and decorate as desired. (See page 21.) Attach the instructions for making the cookies found below.

CHOCOLATE CHUNK TOFFEE COOKIES

Yield:
3 dozen cookies

In addition to the contents of the jar, you will need to add the following ingredients:

½ cup butter, softened

I egg

I teaspoon vanilla extract

Preheat the oven to 375° F. In a large bowl, blend the butter, egg, and vanilla extract. Add the contents of the jar, and stir until well mixed. Drop the dough by heaping teaspoonfuls onto an ungreased baking sheet, spacing the cookies about 2 inches apart. Bake for 10 to 12 minutes, or until the edges are light brown in color. Allow to cool for 2 minutes on the baking sheet. Then transfer to wire racks and cool completely. Serve immediately, or store in an airtight container for up to 1 week.

CHOCOLATEMALTED MILKCRUNCHIES

If you like an old-fashioned malted milkshake,
you're sure to love these chocolate malt treats!

YIELD:
3 DOZEN COOKIES

QUART-SIZE JAR INGREDIENTS

2 cups all-purpose flour

1 1/4 cups malted milk powder

3/4 cup semisweet chocolate chips

1/2 cup sugar

1/2 teaspoon baking powder

1/4 teaspoon salt

ADDITIONAL INGREDIENTS

3/4 cup butter, softened

2 eggs

2 tablespoons water

1. Preheat the oven to 350°F.

2. Place all of the jar ingredients in a medium-sized bowl, and stir until well combined. Set aside.

3. Place the butter, eggs, and water in a large bowl, and blend with a whisk, a fork, or an electric mixer set on low speed.

4. Add the dry ingredients to the butter mixture, and stir with a wooden spoon until well combined.

5. Drop the dough by heaping teaspoonfuls onto an ungreased baking sheet, spacing the cookies about 2 inches apart to allow for spreading.

6. Bake for 14 to 16 minutes, or until the edges are light brown in color. Allow to cool for 2 minutes on the baking sheet. Then transfer to wire racks and cool completely.

7. Serve immediately, or store in an airtight container for up to 1 week.

CREATING THE JAR

3/4 cup semisweet
chocolate chips

1/4 teaspoon salt

1/2 teaspoon baking powder

2 cups all-purpose flour

1 1/4 cups malted milk powder

1/2 cup sugar

1. Wash and thoroughly dry a 1-quart wide-mouth canning jar.

2. Layer the ingredients in the jar as shown at left, pressing firmly with a flat-bottomed object, such as a tart tamper or the bottom of a narrow glass, after each addition. Make the layers as level as possible.

3. Secure the lid, and decorate as desired. (See page 21.) Attach the instructions for making the cookies found below.

Yield:
3 dozen cookies

In addition to the contents of the jar, you will need to add the following ingredients:

3/4 cup butter, softened

2 eggs

2 tablespoons water

CHOCOLATE MALTED MILK CRUNCHIES

Preheat the oven to 350°F. In a large bowl, blend the butter, eggs, and water. Add the contents of the jar, and stir until well mixed. Drop the dough by heaping teaspoonfuls onto an ungreased baking sheet, spacing the cookies about 2 inches apart. Bake for 14 to 16 minutes, or until the edges are light brown in color. Allow to cool for 2 minutes on the baking sheet. Then transfer to wire racks and cool completely. Serve immediately, or store in an airtight container for up to 1 week.

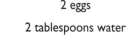

YIELD:
3 DOZEN COOKIES

QUART-SIZE JAR
INGREDIENTS

I cup instant oatmeal

I cup semisweet
chocolate chips

3/4 cup all-purpose
flour

1/2 cup peanut butter-
flavored chips

1/3 cup brown sugar,
packed

1/3 cup sugar

1/2 teaspoon
baking powder

1/8 teaspoon
baking soda

1/8 teaspoon salt

ADDITIONAL
INGREDIENTS

1/2 cup butter,
softened

I egg

I teaspoon
vanilla extract

CHOCOLATEPEANUTBUTTER OATMEALCOOKIES

*My family loves these cookies because they combine some of
our favorite ingredients, including creamy chocolate
and peanut butter chips, and chewy oatmeal.*

1. Preheat the oven to 375°F.

2. Place all of the jar ingredients in a medium-sized bowl, and stir until well combined. Set aside.

3. Place the butter, egg, and vanilla extract in a large bowl, and blend with a whisk, a fork, or an electric mixer set on low speed.

4. Add the dry ingredients to the butter mixture, and stir with a wooden spoon until well combined.

5. Drop the dough by heaping teaspoonfuls onto an ungreased baking sheet, spacing the cookies about 2 inches apart to allow for spreading.

6. Bake for 8 to 10 minutes, or until the edges are light brown in color. Allow to cool for 2 minutes on the baking sheet. Then transfer to wire racks and cool completely.

7. Serve immediately, or store in an airtight container for up to 1 week.

CREATING THE JAR

I cup semisweet chocolate chips

1/2 cup peanut butter-flavored chips

1/3 cup brown sugar, packed

I cup instant oatmeal

1/3 cup sugar

1/2 teaspoon baking powder

1/8 teaspoon baking soda

1/8 teaspoon salt

3/4 cup all-purpose flour

1. Wash and thoroughly dry a 1-quart wide-mouth canning jar.

2. Layer the ingredients in the jar as shown at left, pressing firmly with a flat-bottomed object, such as a tart tamper or the bottom of a narrow glass, after each addition. Make the layers as level as possible.

3. Secure the lid, and decorate as desired. (See page 21.) Attach the instructions for making the cookies found below.

Yield:
3 dozen cookies

In addition to the contents of the jar, you will need to add the following ingredients:

1/2 cup butter, softened

I egg

I teaspoon vanilla extract

CHOCOLATE PEANUT BUTTER OATMEAL COOKIES

Preheat the oven to 375°F. In a large bowl, blend the butter, egg, and vanilla. Add the contents of the jar, and stir until well mixed. Drop the dough by heaping teaspoonfuls onto an ungreased baking sheet, spacing the cookies about 2 inches apart. Bake for 8 to 10 minutes, or until the edges are light brown in color. Allow to cool for 2 minutes on the baking sheet. Then transfer to wire racks and cool completely. Serve immediately, or store in an airtight container for up to 1 week.

COCOADROPS

*My Aunt Phyliss showed me how to make these cookies when I was just
seven years old, and I enjoy them just as much now as I did then.*

YIELD:
3 DOZEN COOKIES

**QUART-SIZE JAR
INGREDIENTS**

2 cups all-purpose
flour

I cup brown sugar,
packed

I cup chopped
walnuts

$^1/_2$ cup cocoa powder

I teaspoon
baking soda

$^1/_2$ teaspoon salt

**ADDITIONAL
INGREDIENTS**

$^1/_2$ cup solid
shortening, such as
Crisco

$^1/_2$ cup milk

2 eggs

I teaspoon
vanilla extract

1. Preheat the oven to 375°F.

2. Place all of the jar ingredients in a medium-sized bowl, and stir
   until well combined. Set aside.

3. Place the shortening, milk, eggs, and vanilla extract in a large bowl,
   and blend with a whisk, a fork, or an electric mixer set on low
   speed.

4. Add the dry ingredients to the shortening mixture, and stir with a
   wooden spoon until well combined.

5. Drop the dough by heaping teaspoonfuls onto an ungreased baking sheet, spacing the cookies about 2 inches apart to allow for
   spreading.

6. Bake for 10 to 12 minutes, or until the edges are light brown in
   color. Allow to cool for 2 minutes on the baking sheet. Then transfer to wire racks and cool completely.

7. Serve immediately, or store in an airtight container for up to 1
   week.

CREATING THE JAR

1 cup chopped walnuts

½ cup cocoa powder

1 cup brown sugar, packed

½ teaspoon salt

1 teaspoon baking soda

2 cups all-purpose flour

1. Wash and thoroughly dry a 1-quart wide-mouth canning jar.

2. Layer the ingredients in the jar as shown at left, pressing firmly with a flat-bottomed object, such as a tart tamper or the bottom of a narrow glass, after each addition. Make the layers as level as possible.

3. Secure the lid, and decorate as desired. (See page 21.) Attach the instructions for making the cookies found below.

Yield:
3 dozen cookies

In addition to the contents of the jar, you will need to add the following ingredients:

½ cup solid shortening, such as Crisco

½ cup milk

2 eggs

1 teaspoon vanilla extract

COCOA DROPS

Preheat the oven to 375°F. In a large bowl, blend the shortening, milk, eggs, and vanilla extract. Add the contents of the jar, and stir until well mixed. Drop the dough by heaping teaspoonfuls onto an ungreased baking sheet, spacing the cookies about 2 inches apart. Bake for 10 to 12 minutes, or until the edges are light brown in color. Allow to cool for 2 minutes on the baking sheet. Then transfer to wire racks and cool completely. Serve immediately, or store in an airtight container for up to 1 week.

COCONUTMACAROONS

*My best friend, Di, makes these delicious cookies and serves them
with a light raspberry sorbet. What an easy, elegant dessert.
Even the gift jar is a snap to make!*

YIELD:
3 DOZEN COOKIES

QUART-SIZE JAR
INGREDIENTS

5 1/3 cups sweetened
flaked coconut

2/3 cup sugar

1/4 cup plus
2 tablespoons
all-purpose flour

1/4 teaspoon salt

ADDITIONAL
INGREDIENTS

4 egg whites

1 teaspoon
almond extract

1. Preheat the oven to 325°F. Grease and flour a baking sheet, and set aside.

2. Place all of the jar ingredients in a medium-sized bowl, and stir until well combined.

3. Add the egg whites and almond extract to the dry ingredients, and stir with a wooden spoon until well blended.

4. Drop the dough by tablespoonfuls onto the prepared baking sheet, spacing the cookies about 2 inches apart to allow for spreading.

5. Bake for 20 minutes, or until the edges of the cookies are golden brown. Immediately transfer to wire racks and cool completely.

6. Serve immediately, or store in an airtight container for up to 1 week.

CREATING THE JAR

5 1/3 cups sweetened
flaked coconut

2/3 cup sugar

1/4 cup plus 2 tablespoons
all-purpose flour

1/4 teaspoon salt

1. Wash and thoroughly dry a 1-quart wide-mouth canning jar.

2. Layer the ingredients in the jar as shown at left, pressing firmly with a flat-bottomed object, such as a tart tamper or the bottom of a narrow glass, after each addition. Make the layers as level as possible.

3. Secure the lid, and decorate as desired. (See page 21.) Attach the instructions for making the cookies found below.

COCONUT MACAROONS

Yield:
3 dozen cookies

In addition to the contents of
the jar, you will need to add
the following ingredients:

4 egg whites

1 teaspoon almond extract

Preheat the oven to 325°F. Place the contents of the jar in a large bowl, and stir in the egg whites and almond extract until well blended. Drop by tablespoonfuls onto a greased and floured baking sheet, spacing the cookies about 2 inches apart. Bake for 20 minutes, or until the edges are golden brown in color. Immediately transfer to wire racks and cool completely. Serve immediately, or store in an airtight container for up to 1 week.

DEVIL'SFOODCOOKIES

These cookies are not only devilishly good to eat, but also amazingly simple to make. Keep the cake mix on hand, and you'll always be able to create a great last-minute gift jar, too.

Yield:
3 DOZEN COOKIES

QUART-SIZE JAR INGREDIENT

One package (18.25 ounces) devil's food cake mix

ADDITIONAL INGREDIENT

One container (8 ounces) sour cream

1. Preheat the oven to 350°F. Lightly grease a baking sheet, and set aside.

2. Place the cake mix in a large bowl. Stir in the sour cream, and blend well with an electric mixer set on low speed.

3. Drop the dough by heaping teaspoonfuls onto the prepared baking sheet, spacing the cookies about 2 inches apart to allow for spreading.

4. Bake for 10 to 12 minutes, or until the tops appear dry. Allow to cool for 1 minute on the baking sheet. Then transfer to wire racks and cool completely.

5. Serve immediately, or store in an airtight container for up to 1 week.

CREATINGTHE**JAR**

One package (18.25 ounces) devil's food cake mix

1. Wash and thoroughly dry a 1-quart wide-mouth canning jar.

2. Place the cake mix in the jar.

3. Secure the lid, and decorate as desired. (See page 21.) Attach the instructions for making the cookies found below.

DEVIL'S FOOD COOKIES

Yield:
3 dozen cookies

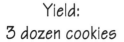

In addition to the contents of the jar, you will need to add the following ingredient:

One container (8 ounces) sour cream

Preheat the oven to 350°F. Place the contents of the jar in a large bowl. Add the sour cream and, using an electric mixer set on low speed, combine until well mixed. Drop the dough by heaping teaspoonfuls onto a lightly greased baking sheet, spacing the cookies about 2 inches apart. Bake for 10 to 12 minutes, or until the tops appear dry. Allow to cool for 1 minute on the baking sheet. Then transfer to wire racks and cool completely. Serve immediately, or store in an airtight container for up to 1 week.

HOLIDAYSPICECOOKIES

*These sweet and spicy cookies are perfect
for the holidays.*

YIELD:
3½ DOZEN
COOKIES

**QUART-SIZE JAR
INGREDIENTS**

2½ cups all-purpose
flour

I cup sugar

I cup brown sugar,
packed

I tablespoon dried,
ground lemon peel

I tablespoon dried,
ground orange peel

I teaspoon cinnamon

I teaspoon
baking soda

½ teaspoon
ground cloves

⅛ teaspoon nutmeg

**ADDITIONAL
INGREDIENTS**

½ cup honey

¼ cup butter,
softened

I egg

2 tablespoons milk

1. Preheat the oven to 350°F.

2. Place all of the jar ingredients in a medium-sized bowl, and stir until well combined. Set aside.

3. Place the honey, butter, egg, and milk in a large bowl, and blend with a whisk, a fork, or an electric mixer set on low speed.

4. Add the dry ingredients to the honey mixture, and stir with a wooden spoon until well combined.

5. Drop the dough by heaping teaspoonfuls onto an ungreased baking sheet, spacing the cookies about 2 inches apart to allow for spreading.

6. Bake for 10 to 12 minutes, or until the edges are light brown in color. Allow to cool for 1 minute on the baking sheet. Then transfer to wire racks and cool completely.

7. Serve immediately, or store in an airtight container for up to 10 days.

CREATING THE JAR

I cup sugar

I cup brown sugar, packed

I teaspoon cinnamon

½ teaspoon ground cloves

⅛ teaspoon ground nutmeg

I tablespoon dried, ground lemon peel

I tablespoon dried, ground orange peel

I teaspoon baking soda

2½ cups all-purpose flour

1. Wash and thoroughly dry a 1-quart wide-mouth canning jar.

2. Layer the ingredients in the jar as shown at left, pressing firmly with a flat-bottomed object, such as a tart tamper or the bottom of a narrow glass, after each addition. Make the layers as level as possible.

3. Secure the lid, and decorate as desired. (See page 21.) Attach the instructions for making the cookies found below.

Yield:
3½ dozen cookies

In addition to the contents of the jar, you will need to add the following ingredients:

½ cup honey

¼ cup butter, softened

I egg

2 tablespoons milk

HOLIDAY SPICE COOKIES

Preheat the oven to 350°F. In a large bowl, blend the honey, butter, egg, and milk. Add the contents of the jar, and stir until well mixed. Drop the dough by heaping teaspoonfuls onto an ungreased baking sheet, spacing the cookies about 2 inches apart. Bake for 10 to 12 minutes, or until the edges are light brown in color. Allow to cool for 1 minute on the baking sheet. Then transfer to wire racks and cool completely. Serve immediately, or store in an airtight container for up to 10 days.

NUTTYCHOCOLATE SNICKERDOODLES

*Cocoa powder gives this old-fashioned favorite
a delicious chocolate twist!*

YIELD:
2½ DOZEN
COOKIES

QUART-SIZE JAR
INGREDIENTS

1¾ cups all-purpose
flour

1½ cups sugar

¾ cup finely ground
pecans

¼ cup cocoa powder

½ teaspoon
baking powder

ADDITIONAL
INGREDIENTS

¾ cup butter,
softened

1 egg

2 teaspoons milk

1 teaspoon
vanilla extract

3 tablespoon sugar

1½ teaspoons
cinnamon

1. Preheat the oven to 375°F.

2. Place all of the jar ingredients in a medium-sized bowl, and stir until well combined. Set aside.

3. Place the butter, egg, milk, and vanilla extract in a large bowl, and blend with a whisk, a fork, or an electric mixer set on low speed.

4. Add the dry ingredients to the butter mixture, and blend with an electric mixer set on medium speed until well combined.

5. Combine the sugar and cinnamon in a small bowl.

6. Roll the dough into 2-inch balls. As each ball is complete, roll it in the sugar mixture and place it on an ungreased baking sheet, spacing the cookies about 2 inches apart to allow for spreading.

7. Bake for 10 to 12 minutes, or until the edges are light brown in color. Allow to cool for 2 minutes on the baking sheet. Then transfer to wire racks and cool completely.

8. Serve immediately, or store in an airtight container for up to 2 weeks.

CREATING THE JAR

3/4 cup finely ground pecans

1 1/2 cups sugar

1/4 cup cocoa powder

1/2 teaspoon baking powder

1 3/4 cups all-purpose flour

1. Wash and thoroughly dry a 1-quart wide-mouth canning jar.

2. Layer the ingredients in the jar as shown at left, pressing firmly with a flat-bottomed object, such as a tart tamper or the bottom of a narrow glass, after each addition. Make the layers as level as possible.

3. Secure the lid, and decorate as desired. (See page 21.) Attach the instructions for making the cookies found below.

Yield:
2 1/2 dozen cookies

In addition to the contents of the jar, you will need to add the following ingredients:

3/4 cup butter, softened

1 egg

2 teaspoons milk

1 teaspoon vanilla extract

3 tablespoons sugar

1 1/2 teaspoons cinnamon

NUTTY CHOCOLATE SNICKERDOODLES

Preheat the oven to 375°F. In a large bowl, blend the butter, egg, milk, and vanilla extract. Add the contents of the jar, and blend with an electric mixer set on medium speed. Combine the sugar and cinnamon. Then roll the dough into 2-inch balls, and roll in the sugar mixture to coat. Place the balls 2 inches apart on an ungreased baking sheet, and bake for 10 to 12 minutes, or until the edges are light brown in color. Allow to cool for 2 minutes on the baking sheet. Then transfer to wire racks and cool completely. Serve immediately, or store in an airtight container for up to 2 weeks.

NUTTYCINNAMONCOOKIES

Although these cookies will be sticky when they're first dusted
with the powdered sugar, once they cool completely,
they'll be dry to the touch and deliciously sweet.

YIELD:
3½ DOZEN
COOKIES

QUART-SIZE JAR
INGREDIENTS

3 cups all-purpose
flour

I cup finely chopped
toasted walnuts
(see page 7)

³/₄ cup
powdered sugar

I teaspoon cinnamon

¹/₄ teaspoon salt

ADDITIONAL
INGREDIENTS

I ¹/₂ cups butter,
softened

I teaspoon
vanilla extract

¹/₂ cup
powdered sugar

1. Preheat the oven to 325°F.

2. Place all of the jar ingredients in a medium-sized bowl, and stir until well combined. Set aside.

3. Place the butter and vanilla extract in a large bowl, and blend with a whisk, a fork, or an electric mixer set on low speed.

4. Add the dry ingredients to the butter mixture, and stir with a wooden spoon until well combined.

5. Roll the dough into 1½-inch balls, and place 2 inches apart on an ungreased baking sheet to allow for spreading.

6. Bake for 15 to 18 minutes, or until the edges are light brown in color. Allow to cool for 5 minutes on the baking sheet. Then roll each cookie in the powdered sugar, coating it completely. Transfer to wire racks and cool completely.

7. Serve immediately, or store in an airtight container for up to 1 week.

CREATINGTHEJAR

1 teaspoon cinnamon

¼ teaspoon salt

1 cup finely chopped toasted walnuts (see page 7)

3 cups all-purpose flour

¾ cup powdered sugar

1. Wash and thoroughly dry a 1-quart wide-mouth canning jar.

2. Layer the ingredients in the jar as shown at left, pressing firmly with a flat-bottomed object, such as a tart tamper or the bottom of a narrow glass, after each addition. Make the layers as level as possible.

3. Secure the lid, and decorate as desired. (See page 21.) Attach the instructions for making the cookies found below.

Yield:
3½ dozen cookies

In addition to the contents of the jar, you will need to add the following ingredients:

1½ cups butter, softened

1 teaspoon vanilla extract

½ cup powdered sugar

NUTTY CINNAMON COOKIES

Preheat the oven to 325° F. In a large bowl, blend the butter and vanilla extract. Add the contents of the jar, and stir until well mixed. Roll the dough into 1½-inch balls and arrange on an ungreased baking sheet, spacing the balls about 2 inches apart. Bake for 15 to 18 minutes, or until the edges are light brown in color. Allow to cool for 5 minutes on the baking sheet. Then roll each cookie in the powdered sugar, and transfer to wire racks to cool completely. Serve immediately, or store in an airtight container for up to 1 week.

OATMEALSCOTCHIES

*These mouth-watering morsels are among
my family's favorite dessert treats.*

YIELD:
3 DOZEN COOKIES

**QUART-SIZE JAR
INGREDIENTS**

1 ½ cups instant
oatmeal

¾ cup butterscotch-
flavored chips

⅔ cup all-purpose
flour

½ cup chopped
walnuts

⅓ cup brown sugar,
packed

⅓ cup sugar

½ teaspoon
baking soda

½ teaspoon
cinnamon

¼ teaspoon salt

**ADDITIONAL
INGREDIENTS**

½ cup butter,
softened

1 egg

1 teaspoon
vanilla extract

1. Preheat the oven to 375° F.

2. Place all of the jar ingredients in a medium-sized bowl, and stir until well combined. Set aside.

3. Place the butter, egg, and vanilla extract in a large bowl, and blend with a whisk, a fork, or an electric mixer set on low speed.

4. Add the dry ingredients to the butter mixture, and stir with a wooden spoon until well combined.

5. Drop the dough by heaping teaspoonfuls onto an ungreased baking sheet, spacing the cookies about 2 inches apart to allow for spreading.

6. Bake for 8 to 10 minutes, or until the edges are light brown in color. Allow to cool for 2 minutes on the baking sheet. Then transfer to wire racks and cool completely.

7. Serve immediately, or store in an airtight container for up to 1 week.

CREATINGTHEJAR

½ cup chopped walnuts

¾ cup butterscotch-flavored chips

⅓ cup brown sugar, packed

1 ½ cups instant oatmeal

½ teaspoon baking soda

½ teaspoon cinnamon

¼ teaspoon salt

⅔ cup all-purpose flour

⅓ cup sugar

1. Wash and thoroughly dry a 1-quart wide-mouth canning jar.

2. Layer the ingredients in the jar as shown at left, pressing firmly with a flat-bottomed object, such as a tart tamper or the bottom of a narrow glass, after each addition. Make the layers as level as possible.

3. Secure the lid, and decorate as desired. (See page 21.) Attach the instructions for making the cookies found below.

Yield:
3 dozen cookies

In addition to the contents of the jar, you will need to add the following ingredients:

½ cup butter, softened

1 egg

1 teaspoon vanilla extract

OATMEAL SCOTCHIES

Preheat the oven to 375°F. In a large bowl, blend the butter, egg, and vanilla extract. Add the contents of the jar, and stir until well mixed. Drop the dough by heaping teaspoonfuls onto an ungreased baking sheet, spacing the cookies about 2 inches apart. Bake for 8 to 10 minutes, or until the edges are light brown in color. Allow to cool for 2 minutes on the baking sheet. Then transfer to wire racks and cool completely. Serve immediately, or store in an airtight container for up to 1 week.

PEANUTBUTTERAND COCOACOOKIES

**YIELD:
3 DOZEN COOKIES**

**QUART-SIZE JAR
INGREDIENTS**

1 ½ cups powdered
sugar

1 ½ cups all-purpose
flour

1 cup brown sugar,
packed

¾ cup cocoa powder

1 teaspoon
baking powder

¼ teaspoon salt

**ADDITIONAL
INGREDIENTS**

½ cup melted butter

½ cup creamy
peanut butter

2 eggs, slightly beaten

1 teaspoon
vanilla extract

*The marriage of chocolate and peanut butter
creates a sublime taste in every bite of this cookie.*

1. Preheat the oven to 350°F.

2. Place all of the jar ingredients in a medium-sized bowl, and stir until well combined. Set aside.

3. Place the butter, peanut butter, eggs, and vanilla extract in a large bowl, and blend with a whisk, a fork, or an electric mixer set on low speed.

4. Add the dry ingredients to the butter mixture, and stir with a wooden spoon until well combined. Note that the dough will be thick.

5. Drop the dough by heaping teaspoonfuls onto an ungreased baking sheet, spacing the cookies about 2 inches apart to allow for spreading.

6. Bake for 10 to 12 minutes, or until the edges are light brown in color. Allow to cool for 5 minutes on the baking sheet. Then transfer to wire racks and cool completely.

7. Serve immediately, or store in an airtight container for up to 10 days.

CREATING THE JAR

1 cup brown sugar, packed

1 ½ cups powdered sugar

¾ cup cocoa powder

1 teaspoon baking powder

¼ teaspoon salt

1 ½ cups all-purpose flour

1. Wash and thoroughly dry a 1-quart wide-mouth canning jar.

2. Layer the ingredients in the jar as shown at left, pressing firmly with a flat-bottomed object, such as a tart tamper or the bottom of a narrow glass, after each addition. Make the layers as level as possible.

3. Secure the lid, and decorate as desired. (See page 21.) Attach the instructions for making the cookies found below.

Yield:
3 dozen cookies

In addition to the contents of the jar, you will need to add the following ingredients:

½ cup melted butter

½ cup creamy peanut butter

2 eggs, slightly beaten

1 teaspoon vanilla extract

PEANUT BUTTER AND COCOA COOKIES

Preheat the oven to 350° F. In a large bowl, blend the butter, peanut butter, eggs, and vanilla extract. Add the contents of the jar, and stir until well mixed. Drop the dough by heaping teaspoonfuls onto an ungreased baking sheet, spacing the cookies about 2 inches apart. Bake for 10 to 12 minutes, or until the edges are light brown in color. Cool for 5 minutes on the baking sheet. Then transfer to wire racks and cool completely. Serve immediately, or store in an airtight container for up to 10 days.

QUART-SIZE JAR
INGREDIENTS

I cup all-purpose
flour

I cup miniature
candy-coated
chocolate pieces,
such as M&M's Mini
Baking Bits

³/₄ cup instant
oatmeal

¹/₂ cup brown sugar,
packed

¹/₂ cup sugar

¹/₂ cup chopped
salted peanuts

¹/₂ teaspoon
baking soda

¹/₄ teaspoon salt

ADDITIONAL
INGREDIENTS

¹/₂ cup butter,
softened

I egg

I teaspoon
vanilla extract

PEANUTTYRAINBOWCOOKIES

*A rainbow of colors makes this peanut-studded cookie
absolutely irresistible.*

1. Preheat the oven to 350°F.

2. Place all of the jar ingredients in a medium-sized bowl, and stir until well combined. Set aside.

3. Place the butter, egg, and vanilla extract in a large bowl, and blend with a whisk, a fork, or an electric mixer set on low speed.

4. Add the dry ingredients to the butter mixture, and stir with a wooden spoon until well combined.

5. Drop the dough by heaping teaspoonfuls onto an ungreased baking sheet, spacing the cookies about 2 inches apart to allow for spreading.

6. Bake for 8 to 10 minutes, or until the edges are light brown in color. Allow to cool for 5 minutes on the baking sheet. Then transfer to wire racks and cool completely.

7. Serve immediately, or store in an airtight container for up to 2 weeks.

CREATING THE JAR

½ cup chopped salted peanuts

½ cup sugar

½ cup brown sugar, packed

1 cup miniature candy-coated chocolate pieces, such as M&M's Mini Baking Bits

¾ cup instant oatmeal

¼ teaspoon salt

½ teaspoon baking soda

1 cup all-purpose flour

1. Wash and thoroughly dry a 1-quart wide-mouth canning jar.

2. Layer the ingredients in the jar as shown at left, pressing firmly with a flat-bottomed object, such as a tart tamper or the bottom of a narrow glass, after each addition. Make the layers as level as possible.

3. Secure the lid, and decorate as desired. (See page 21.) Attach the instructions for making the cookies found below.

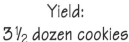

Yield:
3½ dozen cookies

In addition to the contents of the jar, you will need to add the following ingredients:

½ cup butter, softened

1 egg

1 teaspoon vanilla extract

PEANUTTY RAINBOW COOKIES

Preheat the oven to 350°F. In a large bowl, blend the butter, egg, and vanilla extract. Add the contents of the jar, and stir until well mixed. Drop the dough by heaping teaspoonfuls onto an ungreased baking sheet, spacing the cookies about 2 inches apart. Bake for 8 to 10 minutes, or until the edges are light brown in color. Allow to cool for 5 minutes on the baking sheet. Then transfer to wire racks and cool completely. Serve immediately, or store in an airtight container for up to 2 weeks.

PECANSANDIES

With a rich, buttery toffee nut flavor,
these delicate cookies will melt in your mouth.

YIELD:
3 DOZEN COOKIES

QUART-SIZE JAR
INGREDIENTS

2 cups all-purpose
flour

I cup sugar

3/4 cup chopped
pecans

1/2 cup toffee chips

I teaspoon
baking powder

ADDITIONAL
INGREDIENTS

I cup butter, softened

2 egg yolks

1/2 teaspoon
vanilla extract

1. Preheat the oven to 325°F.

2. Place all of the jar ingredients in a medium-sized bowl, and stir until well combined. Set aside.

3. Place the butter, egg yolks, and vanilla extract in a large bowl, and blend with a whisk, a fork, or an electric mixer set on low speed.

4. Add the dry ingredients to the butter mixture, and stir with a wooden spoon until well combined.

5. Roll the dough into 1½-inch balls and place on an ungreased baking sheet, spacing the cookies about 2 inches apart to allow for spreading.

6. Bake for 15 to 17 minutes, or until the edges are very light brown in color. Allow to cool for 5 minutes on the baking sheet. Then transfer to wire racks and cool completely.

7. Serve immediately, or store in an airtight container for up to 10 days.

CREATING THE JAR

3/4 cup chopped pecans

1/2 cup toffee chips

1 teaspoon baking powder

2 cups all-purpose flour

1 cup sugar

1. Wash and thoroughly dry a 1-quart wide-mouth canning jar.

2. Layer the ingredients in the jar as shown at left, pressing firmly with a flat-bottomed object, such as a tart tamper or the bottom of a narrow glass, after each addition. Make the layers as level as possible.

3. Secure the lid, and decorate as desired. (See page 21.) Attach the instructions for making the cookies found below.

Yield:
3 dozen cookies

In addition to the contents of the jar, you will need to add the following ingredients:

1 cup butter, softened

2 egg yolks

1/2 teaspoon vanilla extract

PECAN SANDIES

Preheat the oven to 325°F. In a large bowl, blend the butter, egg yolks, and vanilla extract. Add the contents of the jar, and stir until well mixed. Roll the dough into 1 1/2-inch balls and place on an ungreased baking sheet, spacing the cookies about 2 inches apart. Bake for 15 to 17 minutes, or until the edges are very light brown in color. Allow to cool for 5 minutes on the baking sheet. Then transfer to wire racks and cool completely. Serve immediately, or store in an airtight container for up to 10 days.

PINEAPPLE NUT COOKIES

Take these moist drop cookies to the office or your next potluck supper,
and watch them disappear!

**QUART-SIZE JAR
INGREDIENTS**

1 1/2 cups instant
oatmeal

1 cup all-purpose
flour

1/2 cup brown sugar,
packed

1/2 cup sugar

1/2 cup chopped
walnuts

1/2 teaspoon
baking soda

1/2 teaspoon
cinnamon

1/2 teaspoon salt

**ADDITIONAL
INGREDIENTS**

1/2 cup butter,
softened

1 egg

3/4 cup crushed
pineapple, well
drained

1. Preheat the oven to 375°F.

2. Place all of the jar ingredients in a medium-sized bowl, and stir until well combined. Set aside.

3. Place the butter and egg in a large bowl, and blend with a whisk, a fork, or an electric mixer set on low speed. Then blend in the drained pineapple.

4. Add the dry ingredients to the butter mixture, and stir with a wooden spoon until well combined.

5. Drop the dough by heaping teaspoonfuls onto an ungreased baking sheet, spacing the cookies about 2 inches apart to allow for spreading.

6. Bake for 8 to 10 minutes, or until the edges are light brown in color. Allow to cool for 5 minutes on the baking sheet. Then transfer to wire racks and cool completely.

7. Serve immediately or store on a plate, covered with foil, for up to 3 days. Do *not* store in an airtight container.

CREATING THE JAR

½ cup chopped walnuts

½ cup brown sugar, packed

½ teaspoon salt

½ teaspoon cinnamon

½ teaspoon baking soda

½ cup sugar

1 ½ cups instant oatmeal

1 cup all-purpose flour

1. Wash and thoroughly dry a 1-quart wide-mouth canning jar.

2. Layer the ingredients in the jar as shown at left, pressing firmly with a flat-bottomed object, such as a tart tamper or the bottom of a narrow glass, after each addition. Make the layers as level as possible.

3. Secure the lid, and decorate as desired. (See page 21.) Attach the instructions for making the cookies found below.

Yield:
3 dozen cookies

In addition to the contents of the jar, you will need to add the following ingredients:

½ cup butter, softened

1 egg

¾ cup crushed pineapple, well drained

PINEAPPLE NUT COOKIES

Preheat the oven to 375°F. In a large bowl, blend the butter and egg together until fluffy. Then mix in the pineapple. Add the contents of the jar, and stir until well mixed. Drop the dough by heaping teaspoonfuls onto an ungreased baking sheet, spacing the cookies about 2 inches apart. Bake for 8 to 10 minutes, or until the edges are light brown in color. Allow to cool for 5 minutes on the baking sheet. Then transfer to wire racks and cool completely. Serve immediately or store on a plate, covered with foil, for up to 3 days. For best results, do not use an airtight container.

PINKPOLKA**DOT**COOKIES

Tender, dainty, and delicately colored,
these cookies are the perfect accompaniment to afternoon tea.

YIELD:
3 DOZEN COOKIES

QUART-SIZE JAR
INGREDIENTS

2 cups all-purpose
flour

I cup white
chocolate chips

$^1/_2$ cup brown sugar,
packed

$^1/_2$ cup sugar

$^1/_2$ teaspoon
baking soda

$^1/_2$ teaspoon salt

ADDITIONAL
INGREDIENTS

$^3/_4$ cup buttermilk

8 drops red food
coloring

$^1/_2$ cup solid butter-
flavored shortening,
such as Butter Flavor
Crisco

I egg

I teaspoon
vanilla extract

1. Preheat the oven to 400°F.

2. Place all of the jar ingredients in a medium-sized bowl, and stir until well combined. Set aside.

3. Mix the buttermilk and the red food coloring in a large bowl. Then add the shortening, egg, and vanilla extract, and beat with an electric mixer until well combined.

4. Add the dry ingredients to the buttermilk mixture, and stir with a wooden spoon until well combined.

5. Drop the dough by heaping teaspoonfuls onto an ungreased baking sheet, spacing the cookies about 2 inches apart to allow for spreading.

6. Bake for 9 to 11 minutes, or until the edges are light brown in color. Cool for 3 minutes on the baking sheet. Then transfer to wire racks and cool completely.

7. Serve immediately, or store in an airtight container for up to 10 days.

CREATING THE JAR

1 cup white chocolate chips

½ cup brown sugar, packed

½ cup sugar

½ teaspoon baking soda

½ teaspoon salt

2 cups all-purpose flour

1. Wash and thoroughly dry a 1-quart wide-mouth canning jar.

2. Layer the ingredients in the jar as shown at left, pressing firmly with a flat-bottomed object, such as a tart tamper or the bottom of a narrow glass, after each addition. Make the layers as level as possible.

3. Secure the lid, and decorate as desired. (See page 21.) Attach the instructions for making the cookies found below.

Yield:
3 dozen cookies

In addition to the contents of the jar, you will need to add the following ingredients:

¾ cup buttermilk

8 drops red food coloring

½ cup solid butter-flavored shortening, such as Butter Flavor Crisco

1 egg

1 teaspoon vanilla extract

PINK POLKA DOT COOKIES

Preheat the oven to 400°F. In a large bowl, first mix the buttermilk with the red food coloring; then beat in the shortening, egg, and vanilla extract. Add the contents of the jar, and stir until well mixed. Drop the dough by heaping teaspoonfuls onto an ungreased baking sheet, spacing the cookies about 2 inches apart. Bake for 9 to 11 minutes, or until the edges are light brown in color. Allow to cool for 3 minutes on the baking sheet. Then transfer to wire racks to cool completely. Serve immediately, or store in an airtight container for up to 10 days.

REFRIGERATOR
ALMOND**COOKIES**

**QUART-SIZE JAR
INGREDIENTS**

2 cups all-purpose
flour

I cup sugar

³/₄ cup slivered
almonds

¹/₂ cup brown sugar,
packed

2 teaspoons
baking powder

I teaspoon salt

**ADDITIONAL
INGREDIENTS**

¹/₄ cup butter,
softened

I egg

2 tablespoons milk

I ¹/₂ teaspoons
vanilla extract

*These delicious slice-and-bake cookies require
overnight refrigeration, so plan ahead.*

1. Place all of the jar ingredients in a medium-sized bowl, and stir until well combined. Set aside.

2. Place the butter, egg, milk, and vanilla extract in a large bowl, and blend with a whisk, a fork, or an electric mixer set on low speed.

3. Add the dry ingredients to the butter mixture, and stir with a wooden spoon until well combined.

4. Divide the dough in half, and shape each section into a log that's 1¹/₂ inches in diameter and 6 inches long. Roll in waxed paper and chill overnight.

5. Preheat the oven to 425°F, and grease a baking sheet.

6. Cut the dough into ¹/₈-inch slices and arrange on the prepared baking sheet, spacing the cookies about 2 inches apart to allow for spreading.

7. Bake for 8 to 9 minutes, or until the edges are light brown in color. Allow to cool for 5 minutes on the baking sheet. Then transfer to wire racks and cool completely.

8. Serve immediately, or store in an airtight container for up to 1 week.

CREATING THE JAR

¾ cup slivered almonds

½ cup brown sugar, packed

1 cup sugar

2 teaspoons baking powder

1 teaspoon salt

2 cups all-purpose flour

1. Wash and thoroughly dry a 1-quart wide-mouth canning jar.

2. Layer the ingredients in the jar as shown at left, pressing firmly with a flat-bottomed object, such as a tart tamper or the bottom of a narrow glass, after each addition. Make the layers as level as possible.

3. Secure the lid, and decorate as desired. (See page 21.) Attach the instructions for making the cookies found below.

Yield:
4 dozen cookies

In addition to the contents of the jar, you will need to add the following ingredients:

¼ cup butter, softened

1 egg

2 tablespoons milk

1½ teaspoons vanilla extract

REFRIGERATOR ALMOND COOKIES

In a large bowl, blend the butter, egg, milk, and vanilla extract. Add the contents of the jar, and stir until well mixed. Divide the dough in half, and shape each half into a 6-x-1½-inch log. Roll in waxed paper and chill overnight. Preheat the oven to 425°F. Cut each roll into ⅛-inch slices and place on a greased baking sheet, spacing the cookies about 2 inches apart. Bake for 8 to 9 minutes, or until the edges are light brown in color. Cool for 5 minutes on the baking sheet. Then transfer to wire racks and cool completely. Serve immediately, or store in an airtight container for up to 1 week.

**QUART-SIZE JAR
INGREDIENTS**

1¼ cups all-purpose
flour

1¼ cups graham
cracker crumbs

¾ cup miniature
candy-coated
chocolate pieces,
such as M&M's Mini
Baking Bits

½ cup brown sugar,
packed

½ cup sugar

½ teaspoon
baking soda

¼ teaspoon
cinnamon

**ADDITIONAL
INGREDIENTS**

¾ cup butter,
softened

1 egg

2 tablespoons milk

1 teaspoon
vanilla extract

SWEETCINNAMON GRAHAMCOOKIES

*Graham cracker crumbs are the secret ingredient
that gives this cookie its sweetness.*

1. Preheat the oven to 350°F.

2. Place all of the jar ingredients in a medium-sized bowl, and stir until well combined. Set aside.

3. Place the butter, egg, milk, and vanilla extract in a large bowl, and blend with a whisk, a fork, or an electric mixer set on low speed.

4. Add the dry ingredients to the butter mixture, and stir with a wooden spoon until well combined.

5. Drop the dough by heaping teaspoonfuls onto an ungreased baking sheet, spacing the cookies about 2 inches apart to allow for spreading.

6. Bake for 8 to 10 minutes, or until the edges are light brown in color. Allow to cool for 5 minutes on the baking sheet. Then transfer to wire racks and cool completely.

7. Serve immediately, or store in an airtight container for up to 10 days.

CREATING THE JAR

3/4 cup miniature candy-coated chocolate pieces, such as M&M's Mini Baking Bits

1 1/4 cups graham cracker crumbs

1/4 teaspoon cinnamon

1/2 teaspoon baking soda

1 1/4 cups all-purpose flour

1/2 cup sugar

1/2 cup brown sugar, packed

1. Wash and thoroughly dry a 1-quart wide-mouth canning jar.

2. Layer the ingredients in the jar as shown at left, pressing firmly with a flat-bottomed object, such as a tart tamper or the bottom of a narrow glass, after each addition. Make the layers as level as possible.

3. Secure the lid, and decorate as desired. (See page 21.) Attach the instructions for making the cookies found below.

Yield:
3 1/2 dozen cookies

In addition to the contents of the jar, you will need to add the following ingredients:

3/4 cup butter, softened

1 egg

2 tablespoons milk

1 teaspoon vanilla extract

SWEET CINNAMON GRAHAM COOKIES

Preheat the oven to 350°F. In a large bowl, blend the butter, egg, milk, and vanilla extract. Add the contents of the jar, and stir until well mixed. Drop the dough by heaping teaspoonfuls onto an ungreased baking sheet, spacing the cookies about 2 inches apart. Bake for 8 to 10 minutes, or until the edges are light brown in color. Allow to cool for 5 minutes on the baking sheet. Then transfer to wire racks and cool completely. Serve immediately, or store in an airtight container for up to 10 days.

QUART-SIZE JAR INGREDIENTS

I cup all-purpose flour

I cup instant oatmeal

³/₄ cup sugar

¹/₂ cup dried cherries

¹/₂ cup chopped walnuts

¹/₂ cup white chocolate chips

¹/₂ teaspoon baking powder

¹/₄ teaspoon salt

¹/₈ teaspoon baking soda

ADDITIONAL INGREDIENTS

¹/₂ cup butter, softened

I egg

I teaspoon vanilla extract

WHITECHOCOLATE CHERRYCOOKIES

These delicate little cookies will melt in your mouth. Yum!

1. Preheat the oven to 375°F.

2. Place all of the jar ingredients in a medium-sized bowl, and stir until well combined. Set aside.

3. Place the butter, egg, and vanilla extract in a large bowl, and blend with a whisk, a fork, or an electric mixer set on low speed.

4. Add the dry ingredients to the butter mixture, and stir with a wooden spoon until well combined. Note that the dough will be dry.

5. Roll the dough into 2-inch balls and place on an ungreased baking sheet, spacing the cookies about 2 inches apart to allow for spreading.

6. Bake for 10 to 12 minutes, or until the edges are light brown in color. Allow to cool for 5 minutes on the baking sheet. Then transfer to wire racks and cool completely.

7. Serve immediately, or store in an airtight container for up to 2 weeks.

CREATING THE JAR

½ cup chopped walnuts

½ cup dried cherries

½ cup white chocolate chips

1 cup instant oatmeal

¾ cup sugar

¼ teaspoon salt

⅛ teaspoon baking soda

½ teaspoon baking powder

1 cup all-purpose flour

1. Wash and thoroughly dry a 1-quart wide-mouth canning jar.

2. Layer the ingredients in the jar as shown at left, pressing firmly with a flat-bottomed object, such as a tart tamper or the bottom of a narrow glass, after each addition. Make the layers as level as possible.

3. Secure the lid, and decorate as desired. (See page 21.) Attach the instructions for making the cookies found below.

WHITE CHOCOLATE CHERRY COOKIES

Yield:
3 dozen cookies

In addition to the contents of the jar, you will need to add the following ingredients:

½ cup butter, softened

1 egg

1 teaspoon vanilla extract

Preheat the oven to 375°F. In a large bowl, blend the butter, egg, and vanilla extract. Add the contents of the jar, and stir until well mixed. Roll the dough into 2-inch balls and place on an ungreased baking sheet, spacing the cookies about 2 inches apart. Bake for 10 to 12 minutes, or until the edges are light brown in color. Allow to cool for 5 minutes on the baking sheet. Then transfer to wire racks and cool completely. Serve immediately, or store in an airtight container for up to 2 weeks.

Browniesand Bar**Cookies**

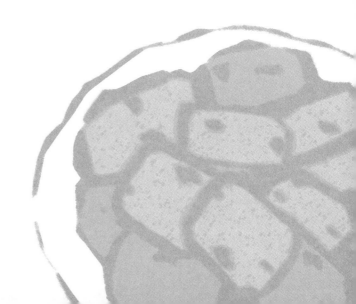

BUTTERSCOTCHBROWNIES

*Here's the perfect dessert for those who love the
chewy sweetness of brownies, but prefer the flavor
of butterscotch to that of traditional chocolate.*

**YIELD:
24 BARS**

**QUART-SIZE JAR
INGREDIENTS**

2 cups all-purpose
flour

1³/₄ cups brown
sugar, packed

¹/₂ cup sugar

1¹/₂ teaspoons
baking powder

¹/₄ teaspoon salt

**ADDITIONAL
INGREDIENTS**

³/₄ cup butter,
softened

2 eggs

2 teaspoons
vanilla extract

1. Preheat the oven to 375°F. Grease a 13-x-9-inch baking pan, and set aside.

2. Place all of the jar ingredients in a medium-sized bowl, and stir until well combined. Set aside.

3. Place the butter, eggs, and vanilla extract in a large bowl, and blend with a whisk, a fork, or an electric mixer set on low speed.

4. Add the dry ingredients to the butter mixture, and stir with a wooden spoon until well combined. The batter will be thick.

5. Spread the batter evenly in the prepared pan, and bake for 20 to 25 minutes, or until a toothpick inserted in the center comes out clean. Allow to cool completely in the pan before cutting into 24 bars.

6. Serve immediately, or store in an airtight container for up to 1 week.

CREATING THE JAR

1¾ cups brown sugar, packed

½ cup sugar

1½ teaspoons baking powder

¼ teaspoon salt

2 cups all-purpose flour

1. Wash and thoroughly dry a 1-quart wide-mouth canning jar.

2. Layer the ingredients in the jar as shown at left, pressing firmly with a flat-bottomed object, such as a tart tamper or the bottom of a narrow glass, after each addition. Make the layers as level as possible.

3. Secure the lid, and decorate as desired. (See page 21.) Attach the instructions for making the bars found below.

Yield:
24 bars

In addition to the contents of the jar, you will need to add the following ingredients:

¾ cup butter, softened

2 eggs

2 teaspoons vanilla extract

BUTTERSCOTCH BROWNIES

Preheat the oven to 375°F. In a large bowl, combine the butter, eggs, and vanilla extract. Add the contents of the jar, and stir until well mixed. Spread the batter evenly in a greased 13-x-9-inch baking pan, and bake for 20 to 25 minutes, or until a toothpick inserted in the center comes out clean. Cool completely in the pan before cutting into 24 squares. Serve immediately, or store in an airtight container for up to 1 week.

EASYCHOCOLATE LOVER'S**BARS**

If you're a chocolate lover like I am,
these bars may well become your favorite dessert!

QUART-SIZE JAR INGREDIENTS

2 cups biscuit mix, such as Bisquick baking mix

I cup brown sugar, packed

¹/₃ cup semisweet chocolate chips

¹/₃ cup white chocolate chips

¹/₃ cup milk chocolate chips

ADDITIONAL INGREDIENTS

¹/₂ cup melted butter

I egg

I teaspoon vanilla extract

1. Preheat the oven to 350°F. Grease an 8-x-8 inch baking pan, and set aside.

2. Place all of the jar ingredients in a medium-sized bowl, and stir until well combined. Set aside.

3. Place the butter, egg, and vanilla extract in a large bowl, and stir to mix well.

4. Add the dry ingredients to the butter mixture, and stir with a wooden spoon just until combined. Do not overstir.

5. Spread the batter evenly in the prepared pan, and bake for 20 to 25 minutes, or until a toothpick inserted in the center comes out clean. Allow to cool completely in the pan before cutting into 16 bars.

6. Serve immediately, or store in an airtight container for up to 1 week.

CREATING THE JAR

¹/₃ cup milk chocolate chips

¹/₃ cup white chocolate chips

¹/₃ cup semisweet
chocolate chips

1 cup brown sugar, packed

2 cups biscuit mix,
such as Bisquick baking mix

1. Wash and thoroughly dry a 1-quart wide-mouth canning jar.

2. Layer the ingredients in the jar as shown at left, pressing firmly with a flat-bottomed object, such as a tart tamper or the bottom of a narrow glass, after each addition. Make the layers as level as possible.

3. Secure the lid, and decorate as desired. (See page 21.) Attach the instructions for making the bars found below.

Yield:
16 bars

In addition to the contents of the jar, you will need to add the following ingredients:

¹/₂ cup melted butter

1 egg

1 teaspoon vanilla extract

Easy Chocolate Lover's Bars

Preheat the oven to 350°F. In a large bowl, combine the butter, egg, and vanilla. Add the contents of the jar, and stir just until well mixed. Do not overstir. Spread the batter evenly in a greased 8-x-8-inch baking pan, and bake for 20 to 25 minutes, or until a toothpick inserted in the center comes out clean. Cool completely in the pan before cutting into 16 squares. Serve immediately, or store in an airtight container for up to 1 week.

MACADAMIANUTBLONDIES

**QUART-SIZE JAR
INGREDIENTS**

1 cup brown sugar,
packed

1 cup all-purpose
flour

1 cup chopped
macadamia nuts

1 cup white
chocolate chips

½ teaspoon
baking soda

⅛ teaspoon salt

**ADDITIONAL
INGREDIENTS**

¾ cup solid butter-
flavored shortening,
such as Butter Flavor
Crisco

1 egg

1 teaspoon
vanilla extract

*My husband, Mike, loves macadamia nut cookies, and says that these
chewy nut-filled bars are twice as nice.*

1. Preheat the oven to 350°F. Grease a 9-x-9-inch baking pan, and set aside.

2. Place all of the jar ingredients in a medium-sized bowl, and stir until well combined. Set aside.

3. Place the shortening, egg, and vanilla extract in a large bowl, and blend with a whisk, a fork, or an electric mixer set on low speed.

4. Add the dry ingredients to the shortening mixture, and stir with a spoon just until combined. Do not overstir.

5. Spread the batter evenly in the prepared pan, and bake for 20 to 25 minutes, or until a toothpick inserted in the center comes out clean. Allow to cool completely in the pan before cutting into 16 bars.

6. Serve immediately, or store in an airtight container for up to 1 week.

CREATING THE JAR

1 cup white chocolate chips

1 cup chopped macadamia nuts

1 cup brown sugar, packed

½ teaspoon baking soda

⅛ teaspoon salt

1 cup all-purpose flour

1. Wash and thoroughly dry a 1-quart wide-mouth canning jar.

2. Layer the ingredients in the jar as shown at left, pressing firmly with a flat-bottomed object, such as a tart tamper or the bottom of a narrow glass, after each addition. Make the layers as level as possible.

3. Secure the lid, and decorate as desired. (See page 21.) Attach the instructions for making the bars found below.

Yield:
16 bars

In addition to the contents of the jar, you will need to add the following ingredients:

¾ cup solid butter-flavored shortening, such as Butter Flavor Crisco

1 egg

1 teaspoon vanilla extract

MACADAMIA NUT BLONDIES

Preheat the oven to 350°F. In a large bowl, blend the shortening, egg, and vanilla extract. Add the contents of the jar, and stir just until well mixed. Do not overstir. Spread the batter evenly in a greased 9-x-9-inch baking pan, and bake for 20 to 25 minutes, or until a toothpick inserted in the center comes out clean. Cool completely in the pan before cutting into 16 squares. Serve immediately, or store in an airtight container for up to 1 week.

NUTTYDOUBLE CHOCOLATEBROWNIES

Who can resist the rich fudgy taste of a chocolate brownie?
And with two kinds of chips, these tempting squares are extra creamy.

YIELD:
16 BARS

QUART-SIZE JAR INGREDIENTS

1 1/4 cups sugar

1 cup all-purpose flour

1/2 cup cocoa powder

1/2 cup semisweet chocolate chips

1/2 cup chopped walnuts

1/3 cup white chocolate chips

1/2 teaspoon baking powder

1/4 teaspoon salt

ADDITIONAL INGREDIENTS

1/2 cup melted butter

3 eggs

1. Preheat the oven to 350°F. Grease an 8-x-8-inch baking pan, and set aside.

2. Place all of the jar ingredients in a medium-sized bowl, and stir until well combined. Set aside.

3. Place the butter and eggs in a large bowl, and stir to mix well.

4. Add the dry ingredients to the butter mixture, and stir just until moistened. Do not overstir.

5. Spread the batter evenly in the prepared pan, and bake for 25 to 30 minutes, or until the brownies begin to pull away from sides of the pan. Allow to cool completely in the pan before cutting into 16 bars.

6. Serve immediately, or store in an airtight container for up to 1 week.

CREATING THE JAR

½ cup chopped walnuts

⅓ cup white chocolate chips

½ cup semisweet chocolate chips

1¼ cups sugar

½ cup cocoa powder

¼ teaspoon salt

½ teaspoon baking powder

1 cup all-purpose flour

1. Wash and thoroughly dry a 1-quart wide-mouth canning jar.

2. Layer the ingredients in the jar as shown at left, pressing firmly with a flat-bottomed object, such as a tart tamper or the bottom of a narrow glass, after each addition. Make the layers as level as possible.

3. Secure the lid, and decorate as desired. (See page 21.) Attach the instructions for making the brownies found below.

NUTTY DOUBLE CHOCOLATE BROWNIES

Yield:
16 bars

In addition to the contents of the jar, you will need to add the following ingredients:

½ cup melted butter

3 eggs

Preheat the oven to 350°F. In a large bowl, combine the butter and eggs. Add the contents of the jar, and stir just until moistened. Do not overstir. Spread the batter evenly in a greased 8-x-8-inch baking pan, and bake for 25 to 30 minutes, or until the brownies begin to pull away from the sides of the pan. Cool completely in the pan before cutting into 16 bars. Serve immediately, or store in an airtight container for up to 1 week.

PEANUTBUTTERS'MORES

*My mom is a peanut butter lover, so when I gave her a pan of these
scrumptious Peanut Butter S'Mores, she ate the whole batch in record
time. Make these for the peanut butter lover in your house!*

**YIELD:
9 BARS**

**QUART-SIZE JAR
INGREDIENTS**

1 ½ cups miniature
marshmallows

1 ½ cups graham
cracker crumbs

1 cup peanut butter
chips

⅓ cup brown sugar,
packed

**ADDITIONAL
INGREDIENTS**

½ cup melted butter

1 teaspoon
vanilla extract

1. Preheat the oven to 350°F. Grease a 9-x-9-inch baking pan, and set aside.

2. Place all of the jar ingredients in a large bowl, and stir until well combined.

3. Pour the butter and vanilla extract over the dry ingredients, and mix with a spoon until well combined.

4. Place the dough in the prepared pan, and use the back of a fork to press it lightly into the pan. Bake for 15 to 18 minutes, or until the top is light brown in color. Allow to cool in the pan for 10 minutes before cutting into 9 bars.

5. Serve immediately, or store in an airtight container for up to 1 week.

CREATING THE JAR

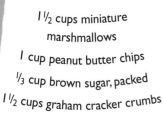

1½ cups miniature marshmallows

1 cup peanut butter chips

⅓ cup brown sugar, packed

1½ cups graham cracker crumbs

1. Wash and thoroughly dry a 1-quart wide-mouth canning jar.

2. Layer the ingredients in the jar as shown at left, pressing firmly with a flat-bottomed object, such as a tart tamper or the bottom of a narrow glass, after each addition. Make the layers as level as possible.

3. Secure the lid, and decorate as desired. (See page 21.) Attach the instructions for making the s'mores found below.

Yield: 9 bars

In addition to the contents of the jar, you will need to add the following ingredients:

½ cup melted butter

1 teaspoon vanilla extract

PEANUT BUTTER S'MORES

Preheat the oven to 350°F. Place the contents of the jar in a large bowl, and stir until well mixed. Pour the butter and vanilla extract over the dry ingredients, and stir to mix. Use the back of a fork to press the dough lightly into a greased 9-x-9-inch baking pan, and bake for 15 to 18 minutes, or until the top is light brown in color. Cool in the pan for 10 minutes before cutting into 9 bars. Serve immediately, or store in an airtight container for up to 1 week.

Muffins,Scones, and**Breads**

APPLEMUFFINS

The aromatic combination of apples, cinnamon, and nutmeg
makes these muffins smell as good as they taste!

YIELD:
15 MUFFINS

PINT-SIZE JAR
INGREDIENTS

2 cups self-rising
flour

I cup chopped
dried apples

1/2 cup sugar

1/4 cup brown sugar,
packed

I teaspoon cinnamon

1/4 teaspoon nutmeg

ADDITIONAL
INGREDIENTS

3/4 cup milk

1/4 cup vegetable oil,
such as canola

I egg

1. Preheat the oven to 400°F.

2. Place all of the jar ingredients in a medium-sized bowl, and stir until well combined. Set aside.

3. Place the milk, oil, and egg in a large bowl, and blend well with a whisk, a fork, or an electric mixer set on low speed.

4. Add the dry ingredients to the milk mixture, and stir with a wooden spoon just until mixed. Do not overstir.

5. Spoon the batter into greased or papered muffin tins, filling each cup about two-thirds full.

6. Bake for 15 to 18 minutes, or until a toothpick inserted in the center of a muffin comes out clean. Allow to cool for 10 minutes in the tin. Then remove the muffins and cool completely on a wire rack.

7. Serve immediately, or store in an airtight container for up to 1 week.

CREATING THE JAR

I cup chopped
dried apples

¹/₄ cup brown sugar, packed

I teaspoon cinnamon

¹/₄ teaspoon nutmeg

¹/₂ cup sugar

2 cups self-rising flour

1. Wash and thoroughly dry a 1-pint wide-mouth canning jar.

2. Layer the ingredients in the jar as shown as left, pressing firmly with a flat-bottomed object, such as a tart tamper or the bottom of a narrow glass, after each addition. Make the layers as level as possible.

3. Secure the lid, and decorate as desired. (See page 21.) Attach the instructions for making the muffins found below.

Yield:
15 muffins

In addition to the contents of the jar, you will need to add the following ingredients:

³/₄ cup milk

¹/₄ cup vegetable oil,
such as canola

I egg

APPLE MUFFINS

Preheat the oven to 400° F. In a large bowl, combine the milk, oil, and egg. Add the contents of the jar, and stir just until mixed. Do not overstir. Spoon the batter into greased or papered muffin tins, filling each cup two-thirds full. Bake for 15 to 18 minutes, or until a toothpick inserted in the center comes out clean. Cool for 10 minutes in the tin. Then transfer to a wire rack and cool completely. Serve immediately, or store in an airtight container for up to 1 week.

BLUEBERRYBANANAMUFFINS

Welcome a new neighbor with a batch of these delicious muffins,
and you'll soon have a new friend.

YIELD:
18 MUFFINS

QUART-SIZE JAR
INGREDIENTS

3 cups all-purpose
flour

I cup sugar

I tablespoon
baking powder

$^1/_2$ teaspoon
baking soda

ADDITIONAL
INGREDIENTS

$^3/_4$ cup milk

$^3/_4$ cup melted butter

2 eggs

I teaspoon
vanilla extract

2 cups
fresh blueberries

I large ripe banana,
mashed

1. Preheat the oven to 375°F.

2. Place all of the jar ingredients in a medium-sized bowl, and stir until well combined. Set aside.

3. Place the milk, butter, eggs, and vanilla extract in a large bowl, and blend well with a whisk, a fork, or an electric mixer set on low speed.

4. Add the dry ingredients to the milk mixture, and stir with a wooden spoon just until mixed. Do not overstir. Then gently fold the blueberries and mashed banana into the batter.

5. Spoon the batter into greased or papered muffin tins, filling each cup about two-thirds full.

6. Bake for 20 minutes, or until a toothpick inserted in the center of a muffin comes out clean. Allow to cool for 10 minutes in the tin. Then remove the muffins and cool completely on a wire rack.

7. Serve immediately, or store in an airtight container for up to 1 week.

CREATINGTHEJAR

3 cups all-purpose flour

1 cup sugar

1 tablespoon baking powder

½ teaspoon baking soda

1. Wash and thoroughly dry a 1-quart wide-mouth canning jar.

2. Layer the ingredients in the jar as shown at left, pressing firmly with a flat-bottomed object, such as a tart tamper or the bottom of a narrow glass, after each addition. Make the layers as level as possible.

3. Secure the lid, and decorate as desired. (See page 21.) Attach the instructions for making the muffins found below.

Yield: 18 muffins

In addition to the contents of the jar, you will need to add the following ingredients:

¾ cup milk

¾ cup melted butter

2 eggs

1 teaspoon vanilla extract

2 cups fresh blueberries

1 large ripe banana, mashed

BLUEBERRY BANANA MUFFINS

Preheat the oven to 375°F. In a large bowl, combine the milk, butter, eggs, and vanilla extract. Add the contents of the jar, and stir just until mixed. Do not overstir. Gently fold in the blueberries and banana. Spoon the batter into greased or papered muffin tins, filling each cup two-thirds full. Bake for 20 minutes, or until a toothpick inserted in the center comes out clean. Cool for 10 minutes in the tin. Then transfer to a wire rack and cool completely. Serve immediately, or store in an airtight container for up to 1 week.

BROWNIECUPS

Take these neat brownies-in-a-cup on your next picnic
for a chocolatey no-mess dessert.

YIELD:
16 MUFFINS

QUART-SIZE JAR
INGREDIENTS

I cup all-purpose
flour

I cup brown sugar,
packed

I cup walnut halves

½ cup sugar

½ cup cocoa powder

ADDITIONAL
INGREDIENTS

3 eggs

I cup melted butter

I teaspoon
vanilla extract

1. Preheat the oven to 350°F.

2. Place all of the jar ingredients in a medium-sized bowl, and stir until well combined. Set aside.

3. Place the eggs in a large bowl, and whisk with a fork. Add the butter and vanilla extract, and continue to whisk until well combined.

4. Add the dry ingredients to the butter mixture, and stir with a wooden spoon just until mixed. Do not overstir.

5. Spoon the batter into greased or papered muffin tins, filling each cup about two-thirds full.

6. Bake for 20 to 25 minutes, or until the tops begin to crack and appear dry. Allow to cool for 10 minutes in the tin. Then remove the muffins and cool completely on a wire rack.

7. Serve immediately, or store in an airtight container for up to 1 week.

CREATING THE JAR

1 cup all-purpose flour

½ cup cocoa powder

½ cup sugar

1 cup brown sugar, packed

1 cup walnut halves

1. Wash and thoroughly dry a 1-quart wide-mouth canning jar.

2. Layer the ingredients in the jar as shown at left, pressing firmly with a flat-bottomed object, such as a tart tamper or the bottom of a narrow glass, after each addition. Make the layers as level as possible.

3. Secure the lid, and decorate as desired. (See page 21.) Attach the instructions for making the muffins found below.

Yield:
16 muffins

In addition to the contents of the jar, you will need to add the following ingredients:

3 eggs

1 cup melted butter

1 teaspoon vanilla extract

BROWNIE CUPS

Preheat the oven to 350°F. In a large bowl, whisk the eggs. Then add the butter and vanilla extract, and whisk together. Add the contents of the jar, and stir until just mixed. Do not overstir. Spoon the batter into greased or papered muffin tins, filling each cup two-thirds full. Bake for 20 to 25 minutes, or until the tops begin to crack and appear dry. Cool for 10 minutes in the tin. Then transfer to a wire rack and cool completely. Serve immediately, or store in an airtight container for up to 1 week.

CHERRY ALMOND MUFFINS

YIELD:
12 MUFFINS

QUART-SIZE JAR
INGREDIENTS

1 ½ cups all-purpose
flour

1 cup instant oatmeal

½ cup brown sugar,
packed

½ cup chopped
dried cherries

½ cup chopped
almonds

2 teaspoons
baking powder

¼ teaspoon
baking soda

¼ teaspoon salt

ADDITIONAL
INGREDIENTS

1 cup vanilla-flavored
yogurt

¼ cup vegetable oil,
such as canola

1 egg

Instead of picking up a muffin at your local coffee shop
each morning, bake a pan of these and enjoy one with your coffee.
You may never eat a store-bought muffin again!

1. Preheat the oven to 375°F.

2. Place all of the jar ingredients in a medium-sized bowl, and stir until well combined. Set aside.

3. Place the yogurt, oil, and egg in a large bowl, and blend well with a whisk, a fork, or an electric mixer set on low speed.

4. Add the dry ingredients to the yogurt mixture, and stir with a wooden spoon just until mixed. Do not overstir.

5. Spoon the batter into greased or papered muffin tins, filling each cup about two-thirds full.

6. Bake for 20 to 25 minutes, or until a toothpick inserted in the center of a muffin comes out clean. Allow to cool for 10 minutes in the tin. Then remove the muffins and cool completely on a wire rack.

7. Serve immediately, or store in an airtight container for up to 1 week.

CREATING THE JAR

½ cup chopped almonds

½ cup chopped dried cherries

½ cup brown sugar, packed

1 cup instant oatmeal

¼ teaspoon salt

¼ teaspoon baking soda

2 teaspoons baking powder

1½ cups all-purpose flour

1. Wash and thoroughly dry a 1-quart wide-mouth canning jar.

2. Layer the ingredients in the jar as shown at left, pressing firmly with a flat-bottomed object, such as a tart tamper or the bottom of a narrow glass, after each addition. Make the layers as level as possible.

3. Secure the lid, and decorate as desired. (See page 21.) Attach the instructions for making the muffins found below.

Yield:
12 muffins

In addition to the contents of the jar, you will need to add the following ingredients:

1 cup vanilla-flavored yogurt

¼ cup vegetable oil, such as canola

1 egg

CHERRY ALMOND MUFFINS

Preheat the oven to 375° F. In a large bowl, combine the yogurt, oil, and egg. Add the contents of the jar, and stir until just mixed. Do not overstir. Spoon the batter into greased or papered muffin tins, filling each cup two-thirds full. Bake for 20 to 25 minutes, or until a toothpick inserted in the center comes out clean. Cool for 10 minutes in the tin. Then transfer to a wire rack and cool completely. Serve immediately, or store in an airtight container for up to 1 week.

DRIEDBLUEBERRYMUFFINS

I love blueberry muffins, so when fresh berries are out of season,
I enjoy these delectable treats.

YIELD:
20 MUFFINS

QUART-SIZE JAR
INGREDIENTS

2¹/₂ cups all-purpose
flour

I cup dried
blueberries

¹/₂ cup sugar

2¹/₂ teaspoons
baking powder

¹/₂ teaspoon
baking soda

¹/₄ teaspoon salt

ADDITIONAL
INGREDIENTS

I cup buttermilk

¹/₂ cup melted butter

2 eggs

I teaspoon
vanilla extract

1. Preheat the oven to 375°F.

2. Place all of the jar ingredients in a medium-sized bowl, and stir until well combined. Set aside.

3. Place the buttermilk, butter, eggs, and vanilla extract in a large bowl, and blend well with a whisk, a fork, or an electric mixer set on low speed.

4. Add the dry ingredients to the buttermilk mixture, and stir with a wooden spoon just until mixed. Do not overstir.

5. Spoon the batter into greased or papered muffin tins, filling each cup about two-thirds full.

6. Bake for 15 to 18 minutes, or until a toothpick inserted in the center of a muffin comes out clean. Allow to cool for 10 minutes in the tin. Then remove the muffins and cool completely on a wire rack.

7. Serve immediately, or store in an airtight container for up to 1 week.

1 cup dried blueberries

¼ teaspoon salt

½ teaspoon baking soda

2½ teaspoons baking powder

2½ cups all-purpose flour

½ cup sugar

CREATING THE JAR

1. Wash and thoroughly dry a 1-quart wide-mouth canning jar.

2. Layer the ingredients in the jar as shown at left, pressing firmly with a flat-bottomed object, such as a tart tamper or the bottom of a narrow glass, after each addition. Make the layers as level as possible.

3. Secure the lid, and decorate as desired. (See page 21.) Attach the instructions for making the muffins found below.

Yield:
20 muffins

In addition to the contents of the jar, you will need to add the following ingredients:

1 cup buttermilk

½ cup melted butter

2 eggs

1 teaspoon vanilla extract

DRIED BLUEBERRY MUFFINS

Preheat the oven to 375°F. In a large bowl, combine the buttermilk, butter, eggs, and vanilla. Add the contents of the jar, and stir just until mixed. Do not overstir. Spoon the batter into greased or papered muffin tins, filling each cup two-thirds full. Bake for 15 to 18 minutes, or until a toothpick inserted in the center comes out clean. Cool for 10 minutes in the tin. Then transfer to a wire rack and cool completely. Serve immediately, or store in an airtight container for up to 1 week.

MARSHMALLOWMUFFINS

*These deliciously sweet and gooey muffins
are guaranteed to be a family favorite.*

YIELD:
12 MUFFINS

QUART-SIZE JAR
INGREDIENTS

2 cups all-purpose
flour

1/2 cup milk
chocolate chips

1/2 cup cocoa powder

1/2 cup sugar

1/4 cup miniature
marshmallows

3 teaspoons
baking powder

ADDITIONAL
INGREDIENTS

1 1/4 cups milk

5 tablespoons
melted butter

1 egg

1. Preheat the oven to 375°F.

2. Place all of the jar ingredients in a medium-sized bowl, and stir until well combined. Set aside.

3. Place the milk, butter, and egg in a large bowl, and blend well with a whisk, a fork, or an electric mixer set on low speed.

4. Add the dry ingredients to the milk mixture, and stir with a wooden spoon just until mixed. Do not overstir.

5. Spoon the batter into greased or papered muffin tins, filling each cup about two-thirds full.

6. Bake for 20 to 25 minutes, or until a toothpick inserted in the center of a muffin comes out clean. Allow to cool for 10 minutes in the tin. Then remove the muffins and cool completely on a wire rack.

7. Serve immediately, or store in an airtight container for up to 1 week.

CREATINGTHEJAR

½ cup milk chocolate chips

¼ cup miniature marshmallows

½ cup sugar

½ cup cocoa powder

3 teaspoons baking powder

2 cups all-purpose flour

1. Wash and thoroughly dry a 1-quart wide-mouth canning jar.

2. Layer the ingredients in the jar as shown at left, pressing firmly with a flat-bottomed object, such as a tart tamper or the bottom of a narrow glass, after each addition. Make the layers as level as possible.

3. Secure the lid, and decorate as desired. (See page 21.) Attach the instructions for making the muffins found below.

Yield:
12 muffins

In addition to the contents of the jar, you will need to add the following ingredients:

1¼ cups milk

5 tablespoons melted butter

1 egg

MARSHMALLOW MUFFINS

Preheat the oven to 375°F. In a large bowl, combine the milk, butter, and egg. Add the contents of the jar, and stir just until mixed. Do not overstir. Spoon the batter into greased or papered muffin tins, filling each cup two-thirds full. Bake for 20 to 25 minutes, or until a toothpick inserted in the center comes out clean. Cool for 10 minutes in the tin. Then transfer to a wire rack and cool completely. Serve immediately, or store in an airtight container for up to 1 week.

RAISINWALNUTMUFFINS

YIELD:
18 MUFFINS

**QUART-SIZE JAR
INGREDIENTS**

2 cups all-purpose
flour

1 ¼ cups sugar

½ cup chopped
walnuts

½ cup dark raisins

1 tablespoon
baking powder

2 teaspoons
cinnamon

½ teaspoon salt

¼ teaspoon
baking soda

**ADDITIONAL
INGREDIENTS**

1 cup melted butter

2 eggs

2 teaspoons
vanilla extract

*If you love the sweetness of raisins and the crunch of walnuts,
these muffins are for you!*

1. Preheat the oven to 400°F.

2. Place all of the jar ingredients in a medium-sized bowl, and stir until well combined. Set aside.

3. Place the butter, eggs, and vanilla extract in a large bowl, and blend well with a whisk, a fork, or an electric mixer set on low speed.

4. Add the dry ingredients to the butter mixture, and stir with a wooden spoon just until mixed. Do not overstir.

5. Spoon the batter into greased or papered muffin tins, filling each cup about two-thirds full.

6. Bake for 20 minutes, or until a toothpick inserted in the center of a muffin comes out clean. Allow to cool for 10 minutes in the tin. Then remove the muffins and cool completely on a wire rack.

7. Serve immediately, or store in an airtight container for up to 1 week.

CREATINGTHEJAR

½ cup dark raisins

½ cup chopped walnuts

2 cups all-purpose flour

1 tablespoon baking powder

¼ teaspoon baking soda

2 teaspoons cinnamon

½ teaspoon salt

1¼ cups sugar

1. Wash and thoroughly dry a 1-quart wide-mouth canning jar.

2. Layer the ingredients in the jar as shown at left, pressing firmly with a flat-bottomed object, such as a tart tamper or the bottom of a narrow glass, after each addition. Make the layers as level as possible.

3. Secure the lid, and decorate as desired. (See page 21.) Attach the instructions for making the muffins found below.

Yield: 18 muffins

In addition to the contents of the jar, you will need to add the following ingredients:

1 cup melted butter

2 eggs

2 teaspoons vanilla extract

RAISIN WALNUT MUFFINS

Preheat the oven to 400°F. In a large bowl, combine the butter, eggs, and vanilla extract. Add the contents of the jar, and stir just until mixed. Do not overstir. Spoon the batter into greased or papered muffin tins, filling each cup two-thirds full. Bake for 20 minutes, or until a toothpick inserted in the center of a muffin comes out clean. Cool for 10 minutes in the tin. Then transfer to a wire rack and cool completely. Serve immediately, or store in an airtight container for up to 1 week.

CRANBERRYWALNUTSCONES

A popular accompaniment to hot beverages, scones are similar to biscuits in texture, but are sweeter in taste. These cranberry-and-walnut-studded treats are perfect for breakfast, dessert, and, of course, afternoon tea.

YIELD:
8 SCONES

QUART-SIZE JAR
INGREDIENTS

2 cups all-purpose
flour

³/₄ cup sweetened
dried cranberries

³/₄ cup chopped
walnuts

2 tablespoons sugar

2 teaspoons
baking powder

I teaspoon nutmeg

¹/₂ teaspoon
baking soda

¹/₂ teaspoon salt

ADDITIONAL
INGREDIENTS

¹/₂ cup cold butter

³/₄ cup buttermilk

I egg, separated

2 teaspoons sugar

1. Preheat the oven to 375°F. Lightly grease a cookie sheet.

2. Place all of the jar ingredients in a large bowl, and stir until well combined.

3. Using a pastry blender or fork, cut the butter into the flour mixture until it resembles coarse crumbs.

4. In a small bowl, combine the buttermilk and egg yolk, blending well. Stir the buttermilk mixture into the flour mixture just until moistened.

5. Turn the dough onto the greased cookie sheet, and use the back of a wooden spoon to pat it into an 8-inch round. Score the round into 8 wedges. Do not cut all the way through the dough.

6. In a small bowl, beat the egg white slightly. Brush the egg over the top of the dough, and sprinkle with the sugar.

7. Bake for 15 to 20 minutes, or until golden brown. Allow to cool for 5 minutes on the baking sheet before cutting into 8 scones. Serve warm, or cool completely and store in an airtight container for up to 1 week.

CREATINGTHEJAR

3/4 cup sweetened
dried cranberries

3/4 cup chopped walnuts

2 tablespoons sugar

2 teaspoons baking powder

I teaspoon nutmeg

1/2 teaspoon baking soda

1/2 teaspoon salt

2 cups all-purpose flour

1. Wash and thoroughly dry a 1-quart wide-mouth canning jar.

2. Layer the ingredients in the jar as shown at left, pressing firmly with a flat-bottomed object, such as a tart tamper or the bottom of a narrow glass, after each addition. Make the layers as level as possible

3. Secure the lid, and decorate as desired. (See page 21.) Attach the instructions for making the scones found below.

Yield:
8 scones

In addition to the contents of the jar, you will need to add the following ingredients:

1/2 cup cold butter

3/4 cup buttermilk

I egg, separated

2 teaspoons sugar

CRANBERRY WALNUT SCONES

Preheat the oven to 375°F. Place the contents of the jar in a large bowl, and stir to combine. Using a pastry blender or fork, cut in the butter until mixture resembles coarse crumbs. Stir in the buttermilk and egg yolk to just moisten. Turn the dough onto a greased cookie sheet, and use the back of a wooden spoon to pat into an 8-inch round. Score it into 8 wedges without cutting through. Beat the egg white slightly, and brush over the dough. Sprinkle with the sugar and bake for 15 to 20 minutes, or until golden brown. Cool for 5 minutes, cut into scones, and serve warm; or cool completely and store in container for up to 1 week.

OATANDCHERRYSCONES

YIELD:
12 SCONES

QUART-SIZE JAR
INGREDIENTS

2¹/₂ cups all-purpose
flour

I cup instant oatmeal

I cup dried cherries

¹/₂ cup brown sugar,
packed

2 teaspoons
baking powder

¹/₂ teaspoon
baking soda

¹/₂ teaspoon salt

ADDITIONAL
INGREDIENTS

10 tablespoons
melted butter (¹/₂ cup
plus 2 tablespoons)

²/₃ cup milk

2 eggs

I teaspoon
vanilla extract

I egg white

3 tablespoons water

If you often have scones for breakfast, bake a batch of these oat-and-cherry pastries, wrap them individually, and pop them into the freezer. Then each day, you'll only have to thaw one in the microwave to enjoy a delicious homemade breakfast.

1. Preheat the oven to 375°F. Lightly grease a cookie sheet.

2. Place all of the jar ingredients in a medium-sized bowl, and stir until well combined. Set aside.

3. Place the butter, milk, eggs, and vanilla extract in a large bowl, and blend well with a whisk, a fork, or an electric mixer set on low speed.

4. Add the dry ingredients to the butter mixture, and stir with a wooden spoon just until moistened. Allow the dough to rest for 5 minutes.

5. Divide the dough into two parts, and form each one into a 6-inch round. Place the rounds on the prepared sheet, spacing them about 2 inches apart. Score each round into 6 wedges. Do not cut all the way through the dough.

6. Place the egg white and water in a small bowl and beat well with a fork. Then brush each round with the egg white mixture.

7. Bake for 20 to 25 minutes, or until golden brown. Allow to cool for 5 minutes on the baking sheet before cutting each round into 6 scones. Serve warm, or cool completely and store in an airtight container for up to 1 week.

CREATING THE JAR

1. Wash and thoroughly dry a 1-quart wide-mouth canning jar.

2. Layer the ingredients in the jar as shown at left, pressing firmly with a flat-bottomed object, such as a tart tamper or the bottom of a narrow glass, after each addition. Make the layers as level as possible

3. Secure the lid, and decorate as desired. (See page 21.) Attach the instructions for making the scones found below.

I cup dried cherries

½ cup brown sugar, packed

I cup instant oatmeal

2 teaspoons baking powder

½ teaspoon baking soda

½ teaspoon salt

2½ cups all-purpose flour

Yield: 12 scones

In addition to the contents of the jar, you will need to add the following ingredients:

10 tablespoons melted butter (½ cup plus 2 tablespoons)

⅔ cup milk

2 eggs

I teaspoon vanilla extract

I egg white

3 tablespoons water

OAT AND CHERRY SCONES

Preheat the oven to 375°F. In a large bowl, combine the butter, milk, eggs, and vanilla extract. Add the contents of the jar, and stir until just moistened. Let stand 5 minutes. Shape the dough into two 6-inch rounds, and place on a lightly greased cookie sheet about 2 inches apart. With a floured knife, score each round into 6 wedges without cutting through the dough. Combine the egg white and water, and brush over each round. Bake for 20 to 25 minutes, or until golden brown. Cool for 5 minutes, cut into scones, and serve warm; or cool completely and store in an airtight container for up to 1 week.

BANANANUTBREAD

YIELD:
9-INCH LOAF

QUART-SIZE JAR
INGREDIENTS

2 cups all-purpose
flour

I cup chopped
walnuts

I cup sugar

2 teaspoons
baking powder

I teaspoon salt

$\frac{1}{2}$ teaspoon
baking soda

ADDITIONAL
INGREDIENTS

3 ripe bananas,
mashed

$\frac{1}{2}$ cup solid
shortening, such as
Crisco

$\frac{1}{3}$ cup buttermilk

2 eggs

I love banana bread, and this version is particularly good because the buttermilk gives it a wonderful flavor while making it lusciously moist.

1. Preheat the oven to 350°F. Generously grease a 9-x-5-inch loaf pan and set aside.

2. Place all of the jar ingredients in a medium-sized bowl, and stir until well combined. Set aside.

3. Place the bananas, shortening, buttermilk, and eggs in a large bowl, and blend with a whisk, a fork, or an electric mixer set on low speed.

4. Add the dry ingredients to the banana mixture, and stir with a wooden spoon just until combined. Do not overstir. Pour the batter into the prepared loaf pan.

5. Bake for 45 to 50 minutes, or until a toothpick inserted in the center of the loaf comes out clean. Cool for 10 minutes in the pan. Then remove the bread and cool completely on a wire rack.

6. Serve immediately, or store in an airtight container for up to 1 week.

CREATINGTHEJAR

I cup chopped walnuts

I cup sugar

I teaspoon salt

2 teaspoons baking powder

½ teaspoon baking soda

2 cups all-purpose flour

1. Wash and thoroughly dry a 1-quart wide-mouth canning jar.

2. Layer the ingredients in the jar as shown at left, pressing firmly with a flat-bottomed object, such as a tart tamper or the bottom of a narrow glass, after each addition. Make the layers as level as possible

3. Secure the lid, and decorate as desired. (See page 21.) Attach the instructions for making the bread found below.

Yield:
9-inch loaf

In addition to the contents of the jar, you will need to add the following ingredients:

3 ripe bananas, mashed

½ cup solid shortening, such as Crisco

⅓ cup buttermilk

2 eggs

BANANA NUT BREAD

Preheat the oven to 350°F. In a large bowl, blend the bananas, shortening, buttermilk, and eggs. Add the contents of the jar, and stir just until combined. Do not overstir. Pour the batter into a greased 9-x-5-inch loaf pan. Bake for 45 to 50 minutes, or until a toothpick inserted in the center of the loaf comes out clean. Cool for 10 minutes in the pan, then remove the bread and cool completely on a wire rack. Serve immediately, or store in an airtight container for up to 1 week.

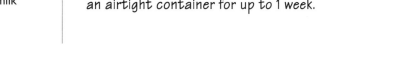

Cakesand **Cupcakes**

BANANASNACKCAKE

Fragrant with ripe bananas, this cake is so moist
and delicious that it needs no icing.

YIELD:
9 SERVINGS

**QUART-SIZE JAR
INGREDIENTS**

2 cups all-purpose
flour

³/₄ cup brown sugar,
packed

³/₄ cup chopped
walnuts

¹/₂ cup sugar

I teaspoon
baking soda

I teaspoon salt

**ADDITIONAL
INGREDIENTS**

I cup mashed ripe
banana

¹/₂ cup buttermilk

¹/₂ cup solid
shortening,
such as Crisco

2 eggs

1. Preheat the oven to 350°F. Generously grease an 8-x-8-inch square baking pan, and set aside.

2. Place all of the jar ingredients in a medium-sized bowl, and stir until well combined. Set aside.

3. Place the banana, buttermilk, shortening, and eggs in a large bowl, and blend with a whisk, a fork, or an electric mixer set on low speed.

4. Add the dry ingredients to the banana mixture, and stir with a wooden spoon until well combined. Pour the batter into the prepared baking pan.

5. Bake for 30 to 35 minutes, or until a toothpick inserted in the center of the cake comes out clean. Allow to cool for 5 minutes in the pan. Then remove from the pan and transfer to a wire rack to cool completely.

6. Serve immediately, or store in an airtight container for up to 1 week.

CREATING THE JAR

3/4 cup chopped walnuts

3/4 cup brown sugar, packed

1/2 cup sugar

1 teaspoon baking soda

1 teaspoon salt

2 cups all-purpose flour

1. Wash and thoroughly dry a 1-quart wide-mouth canning jar.

2. Layer the ingredients in the jar as shown at left, pressing firmly with a flat-bottomed object, such as a tart tamper or the bottom of a narrow glass, after each addition. Make the layers as level as possible.

3. Secure the lid, and decorate as desired. (See page 21.) Attach the instructions for making the cake found below.

Yield:
9 servings

In addition to the contents of the jar, you will need to add the following ingredients:

1 cup mashed ripe banana

1/2 cup buttermilk

1/2 cup solid shortening, such as Crisco

2 eggs

Banana Snack Cake

Preheat the oven to 350°F. In a large bowl, blend the banana, buttermilk, shortening, and eggs. Add the contents of the jar, and stir well. Pour the batter into a generously greased 8-x-8-inch square baking pan and bake for 30 to 35 minutes, or until a toothpick inserted in the center comes out clean. Cool for 5 minutes in the baking pan. Then remove from the pan and transfer to a wire rack to cool completely. Serve immediately, or store in an airtight container for up to 1 week.

CHOCOLATECHIP COFFEECAKE

This chocolate chip-studded cake is a real treat,
and so easy to make that you can enjoy it any time.

YIELD:
12 SERVINGS

QUART-SIZE JAR INGREDIENTS

2½ cups all-purpose flour

1 cup sugar

1 cup semisweet chocolate chips

1½ teaspoons baking powder

1 teaspoon baking soda

1 teaspoon cinnamon

ADDITIONAL INGREDIENTS

2 eggs

1 cup sour cream

½ cup butter, softened

1 teaspoon vanilla extract

1. Preheat the oven to 350°F. Generously grease a 9-x-13-inch baking pan, and set aside.

2. Place all of the jar ingredients in a medium-sized bowl, and stir until well combined. Set aside.

3. Place the eggs, sour cream, butter, and vanilla extract in a large bowl, and blend well with an electric mixer set on low speed.

4. Add the dry ingredients to the egg mixture, and continue beating with the electric mixer for 2 minutes. Pour the batter into the prepared pan.

5. Bake for 25 to 30 minutes, or until a toothpick inserted in the center of the cake comes out clean. Allow to cool for 10 minutes in the pan. Then remove from the pan and transfer to a wire rack to cool completely.

6. Serve immediately, or store in an airtight container for up to 1 week.

CREATING THE JAR

I cup semisweet chocolate chips

I cup sugar

1 1/2 teaspoons baking powder

I teaspoon baking soda

I teaspoon cinnamon

2 1/2 cups all-purpose flour

1. Wash and thoroughly dry a 1-quart wide-mouth canning jar.

2. Layer the ingredients in the jar as shown at left, pressing firmly with a flat-bottomed object, such as a tart tamper or the bottom of a narrow glass, after each addition. Make the layers as level as possible.

3. Secure the lid, and decorate as desired. (See page 21.) Attach the instructions for making the cake found below.

Yield:
12 servings

In addition to the contents of the jar, you will need to add the following ingredients:

2 eggs

I cup sour cream

1/2 cup butter, softened

I teaspoon vanilla extract

CHOCOLATE CHIP COFFEE CAKE

Preheat the oven to 350°F. Place the eggs, sour cream, butter, and vanilla extract in a large bowl, and blend with an electric mixer set on low speed. Add the contents of the jar, and continue to blend for 2 minutes. Pour the batter into a greased 9-x-13-inch baking pan, and bake for 25 to 30 minutes, or until a toothpick inserted in the center of the cake comes out clean. Cool for 10 minutes in the baking pan. Then remove from the pan and transfer to a wire rack to cool completely. Serve immediately, or store in an airtight container for up to 1 week.

PINEAPPLECAKE

Serve this cake plain, or for a truly fabulous dessert,
make a simple glaze and pour it over the hot cake to wow your guests.

YIELD:
16 SERVINGS

QUART-SIZE JAR
INGREDIENTS

2 cups biscuit mix, such
as Bisquick baking mix

I cup all-purpose flour

I cup sugar

I teaspoon
baking soda

ADDITIONAL
INGREDIENTS

¾ cup sour cream

½ cup butter, softened

2 eggs

2 teaspoons
vanilla extract

16-ounce can crushed
pineapple in heavy
syrup, drained (reserve
syrup for glaze)

OPTIONAL GLAZE

¾ cup sugar

¼ cup reserved heavy
syrup from pineapple

¼ cup butter

1. Preheat the oven to 350°F. Generously grease a 9-inch bundt pan, and set aside.

2. Place all of the jar ingredients in a medium-sized bowl, and stir until well combined. Set aside.

3. Place the sour cream, butter, eggs, and vanilla extract in a large bowl, and blend well with an electric mixer set on low speed.

4. Add the dry ingredients to the sour cream mixture, and continue beating with the electric mixer for 2 minutes. Stir in the drained pineapple with a wooden spoon.

5. Pour the batter into the prepared pan and bake for 45 to 50 minutes, or until a toothpick inserted in the center of the cake comes out clean. Allow to cool for 10 minutes in the pan.

6. While the cake is cooling, if a glaze is desired, combine the glaze ingredients in a small saucepan and stir over low heat until the butter is melted and the sugar is dissolved .

7. Transfer the cake to a plate and, if using, pour the warm glaze over the top. Serve immediately, or cover and store for up to 1 week.

CREATING THE JAR

1 cup sugar

1 cup all-purpose flour

1 teaspoon baking soda

2 cups biscuit mix, such as Bisquick baking mix

1. Wash and thoroughly dry a 1-quart wide-mouth canning jar.

2. Layer the ingredients in the jar as shown at left, pressing firmly with a flat-bottomed object, such as a tart tamper or the bottom of a narrow glass, after each addition. Make the layers as level as possible

3. Secure the lid, and decorate as desired. (See page 21.) Attach the instructions for making the cake found below.

Yield: 16 servings

In addition to the contents of the jar, you will need to add:

³/₄ cup sour cream

¹/₂ cup butter, softened

2 eggs

2 teaspoons vanilla extract

16-ounce can crushed pineapple in heavy syrup, drained

OPTIONAL GLAZE

³/₄ cup sugar

¹/₄ cup reserved heavy syrup from pineapple

¹/₄ cup butter

PINEAPPLE CAKE

Preheat the oven to 350°F. In a large bowl, combine the sour cream, butter, eggs, and vanilla extract, and blend with an electric mixer set on low speed. Add the contents of the jar, and continue to blend for 2 minutes. Stir in the drained pineapple. Pour the batter into a generously greased 9-inch bundt pan and bake for 45 to 50 minutes, or until a toothpick inserted in the center of the cake comes out clean. Cool for 10 minutes in the pan. If glaze is desired, stir glaze ingredients over low heat until combined and heated. Transfer warm cake to plate and pour glaze over top. Serve immediately, or cover and store for up to 1 week.

APPLESAUCECUPCAKES

YIELD:
24 CUPCAKES

QUART-SIZE JAR INGREDIENTS

2 cups all-purpose flour

1 1/2 cups sugar

1 cup chopped pecans

1 1/2 teaspoons nutmeg

1 teaspoon cinnamon

1/2 teaspoon ground cloves

1/4 teaspoon salt

ADDITIONAL INGREDIENTS

1 1/2 cups applesauce

2 teaspoons baking soda

3/4 cup melted butter

1 egg

1 teaspoon vanilla extract

Want to use up that last portion or two of applesauce left in the fridge? Whip up a batch of these moist cupcakes and enjoy them for dessert, as a lunchtime treat, or as a sweet snack.

1. Preheat the oven to 350°F.

2. Place all of the jar ingredients in a medium-sized bowl, and stir until well combined. Set aside.

3. Place the applesauce in a small bowl and microwave for 45 seconds on high power. Stir in the baking soda and set aside.

4. In a large bowl, combine the butter, egg, and vanilla extract.

5. Add the dry ingredients to the butter mixture, and mix well with a wooden spoon. Then stir in the applesauce.

6. Spoon the batter into papered muffin tins, filling each liner half full.

7. Bake for 20 to 25 minutes, or until a toothpick inserted in the center of a cupcake comes out clean. Allow to cool for 5 minutes in the tin. Then remove the cupcakes and cool completely on a wire rack.

8. Serve immediately, or store in an airtight container for up to 1 week.

CREATING THE JAR

1 cup chopped pecans

1 ½ teaspoons nutmeg

1 teaspoon cinnamon

½ teaspoon ground cloves

¼ teaspoon salt

2 cups all-purpose flour

1 ½ cups sugar

1. Wash and thoroughly dry a 1-quart wide-mouth canning jar.

2. Layer the ingredients in the jar as shown at left, pressing firmly with a flat-bottomed object, such as a tart tamper or the bottom of a narrow glass, after each addition. Make the layers as level as possible.

3. Secure the lid, and decorate as desired. (See page 21.) Attach the instructions for making the cupcakes found below.

Yield:
24 cupcakes

In addition to the contents of the jar, you will need to add the following ingredients:

1 ½ cups applesauce

2 teaspoons baking soda

¾ cup melted butter

1 egg

1 teaspoon vanilla extract

APPLESAUCE CUPCAKES

Preheat the oven to 350°F. Microwave the applesauce for 45 seconds, and immediately stir in the baking soda. Set aside. In a large bowl, combine the butter, egg, and vanilla extract. Add the contents of the jar, and stir until well mixed. Stir in the applesauce mixture. Spoon the batter into papered muffin tins, filling each liner half full. Bake for 20 to 25 minutes, or until a toothpick inserted in the center comes out clean. Cool for 5 minutes in the tin. Then transfer to a wire rack and cool completely. Serve immediately, or store in an airtight container for up to 1 week.

YIELD:
20 CUPCAKES

CHOCOLATECHIP COOKIECUPCAKES

If you're crazy about chocolate chip cookies, be prepared to fall in love.
These chip-filled cupcakes are so rich that no frosting is needed.

QUART-SIZE JAR
INGREDIENTS

1 ½ cups all-purpose
flour

1 cup semisweet
chocolate chips

¾ cup sugar

¾ cup brown sugar,
packed

¾ teaspoon
baking powder

½ teaspoon salt

ADDITIONAL
INGREDIENTS

1 cup butter, softened

3 eggs

⅓ cup milk

1 teaspoon
vanilla extract

1. Preheat the oven to 375°F.

2. Place all of the jar ingredients in a medium-sized bowl, and stir until well combined. Set aside.

3. Place the butter, eggs, milk, and vanilla extract in a large bowl, and blend well with an electric mixer set on low speed.

4. Add the dry ingredients to the butter mixture, and continue beating with an electric mixer for 2 minutes.

5. Spoon the batter into papered muffin tins, filling each liner half full.

6. Bake for 17 to 20 minutes, or until a toothpick inserted in the center of a cupcake comes out clean. Allow to cool for 5 minutes in the tin. Then remove the cupcakes and cool completely on a wire rack.

7. Serve immediately, or store in an airtight container for up to 5 days.

CREATING THE JAR

I cup semisweet
chocolate chips

¾ cup brown sugar, packed

¾ cup sugar

¾ teaspoon baking powder

½ teaspoon salt

I ½ cups all-purpose flour

1. Wash and thoroughly dry a 1-quart wide-mouth canning jar.

2. Layer the ingredients in the jar as shown at left, pressing firmly with a flat-bottomed object, such as a tart tamper or the bottom of a narrow glass, after each addition. Make the layers as level as possible

3. Secure the lid, and decorate as desired. (See page 21.) Attach the instructions for making the cupcakes found below.

Yield:
20 cupcakes

In addition to the contents of the jar, you will need to add the following ingredients:

I cup butter, softened

3 eggs

⅓ cup milk

I teaspoon vanilla extract

CHOCOLATE CHIP COOKIE CUPCAKES

Preheat the oven to 375°F. In a large bowl, combine the butter, eggs, milk, and vanilla extract, and blend with an electric mixer set on low speed. Add the contents of the jar, and continue to blend for 2 minutes. Spoon the batter into papered muffin tins, filling each liner half full. Bake for 17 to 20 minutes, or until a toothpick inserted in the center comes out clean. Cool for 5 minutes in the tin. Then transfer to a wire rack and cool completely. Serve immediately, or store in an airtight container for up to 5 days.

PEANUTBUTTERCUPCAKES

QUART-SIZE JAR
INGREDIENTS

1³/₄ cups all-purpose
flour

1¹/₃ cups sugar

1 cup peanut butter-
flavored chips

³/₄ teaspoon
baking powder

¹/₂ teaspoon salt

¹/₄ teaspoon
baking soda

ADDITIONAL
INGREDIENTS

³/₄ cup solid butter-
flavored shortening,
such as Butter Flavor
Crisco

²/₃ cup creamy
peanut butter

3 eggs

¹/₂ cup milk

¹/₂ teaspoon
vanilla extract

Enjoy these cupcakes as is, or top with your favorite
chocolate frosting for a party-perfect treat.

1. Preheat the oven to 375°F.

2. Place all of the jar ingredients in a medium-sized bowl, and stir until well combined. Set aside.

3. Place the shortening, peanut butter, eggs, milk, and vanilla extract in a large bowl, and blend well with an electric mixer set on low speed.

4. Add the dry ingredients to the shortening mixture, and beat with the mixer set on medium speed for 2 minutes.

5. Spoon the batter into papered muffin tins, filling each liner half full.

6. Bake for 15 to 18 minutes, or until a toothpick inserted in the center of a cupcake comes out clean. Allow to cool for 5 minutes in the tin. Then remove the cupcakes and cool completely on a wire rack.

7. Serve immediately, or store in an airtight container for up to 5 days.

CREATING THE JAR

1. Wash and thoroughly dry a 1-quart wide-mouth canning jar.

2. Layer the ingredients in the jar as shown at left, pressing firmly with a flat-bottomed object, such as a tart tamper or the bottom of a narrow glass, after each addition. Make the layers as level as possible

3. Secure the lid, and decorate as desired. (See page 21.) Attach the instructions for making the cupcakes found below.

1 cup peanut butter-flavored chips

1 1/3 cups sugar

3/4 teaspoon baking powder

1/2 teaspoon salt

1/4 teaspoon baking soda

1 3/4 cups all-purpose flour

Yield: 24 cupcakes

In addition to the contents of the jar, you will need to add the following ingredients:

3/4 cup solid butter-flavored shortening, such as Butter Flavor Crisco

2/3 cup creamy peanut butter

3 eggs

1/2 cup milk

1/2 teaspoon vanilla extract

PEANUT BUTTER CUPCAKES

Preheat the oven to 375°F. In a large bowl, combine the shortening, peanut butter, eggs, milk, and vanilla extract, and blend with an electric mixer set on low speed. Add the contents of the jar, and continue to blend for 2 minutes. Spoon the batter into papered muffin tins, filling each liner half full. Bake for 15 to 18 minutes, or until a toothpick inserted in the center comes out clean. Cool for 5 minutes in the tin. Then transfer to a wire rack and cool completely. Serve immediately, or store in an airtight container for up to 5 days.

RAINBOWCUPCAKES

These colorful cupcakes are a great alternative to traditional birthday cake. Just top with your favorite frosting.

Yɪᴇʟᴅ:
24 CUPCAKES

QUART-SIZE JAR INGREDIENTS

2¼ cups all-purpose flour

1⅔ cups sugar

1 cup miniature candy-coated chocolate pieces, such as M&M's Mini Baking Bits

1 tablespoon baking powder

½ teaspoon salt

ADDITIONAL INGREDIENTS

3 large egg whites

1 cup milk

½ cup butter, softened

2 teaspoons vanilla extract

1. Preheat the oven to 350°F.

2. Place all of the jar ingredients in a medium-sized bowl, and stir until well combined. Set aside.

3. Place the egg whites, milk, butter, and vanilla extract in a large bowl, and blend well with an electric mixer set on medium speed for 2 minutes.

4. Add the dry ingredients to the egg mixture, and blend on low speed for 2 more minutes.

5. Spoon the batter into papered muffin tins, filling each liner two-thirds full.

6. Bake for 20 to 25 minutes, or until a toothpick inserted in the center of a cupcake comes out clean. Allow to cool for 5 minutes in the tin. Then remove the cupcakes and cool completely on a wire rack.

7. Serve immediately, or store in an airtight container for up to 1 week.

CREATING THE JAR

1²/₃ cups sugar

1 cup miniature candy-coated chocolate pieces, such as M&M's Mini Baking Bits

1 tablespoon baking powder

¹/₂ teaspoon salt

2¹/₄ cups all-purpose flour

1. Wash and thoroughly dry a 1-quart wide-mouth canning jar.

2. Layer the ingredients in the jar as shown at left, pressing firmly with a flat-bottomed object, such as a tart tamper or the bottom of a narrow glass, after each addition.

3. Secure the lid, and decorate as desired. (See page 21.) Attach the instructions for making the cupcakes found below.

Yield:
24 cupcakes

In addition to the contents of the jar, you will need to add the following ingredients:

3 large egg whites

1 cup milk

¹/₂ cup butter, softened

2 teaspoons vanilla extract

RAINBOW CUPCAKES

Preheat the oven to 350°F. In a large bowl, combine the egg whites, milk, butter, and vanilla extract, and blend with an electric mixer set on medium speed for 2 minutes. Add the contents of the jar, and blend on low speed for 2 minutes. Spoon the batter into papered muffin tins, filling each liner two-thirds full. Bake for 20 to 25 minutes, or until a toothpick inserted in the center comes out clean. Cool for 5 minutes in the tin. Then transfer to a wire rack and cool completely. Serve immediately, or store in an airtight container for up to 1 week.

CHOCOLATE SHORTCAKES

Top each square of this cake with sliced fresh strawberries that have been sprinkled with sugar and allowed to stand for about an hour— just until the berries give off their juice. Then add a dollop of whipped cream for a chocolatey twist on a classic summertime dessert.

YIELD:
12 SHORTCAKES

QUART-SIZE JAR INGREDIENTS

2 cups cake flour

1 ½ cups sugar

⅔ cup cocoa powder

1 ½ teaspoons baking soda

1 teaspoon salt

ADDITIONAL INGREDIENTS

1 ½ cups buttermilk

2 eggs

½ cup solid shortening, such as Crisco

1 teaspoon vanilla extract

1. Preheat the oven to 350°F. Generously grease a 9-x-13-inch baking pan, and set aside.

2. Place all of the jar ingredients in a medium-sized bowl, and stir until well combined. Set aside.

3. Place the buttermilk, eggs, shortening, and vanilla extract in a large bowl, and blend with an electric mixer set on low speed for 30 seconds.

4. Add the dry ingredients to the buttermilk mixture, and continue beating with the mixer for 3 minutes. Pour the batter into the prepared baking pan.

5. Bake for 25 to 30 minutes, or until a toothpick inserted in the center of the cake comes out clean. Allow to cool completely in the pan.

6. Cut into 12 squares and serve immediately, topped with strawberries and whipped cream, or store in an airtight container for up to 1 week.

CREATING THE JAR

2/3 cup cocoa powder

1 1/2 teaspoons baking soda

1 teaspoon salt

2 cups cake flour

1 1/2 cups sugar

1. Wash and thoroughly dry a 1-quart wide-mouth canning jar.

2. Loosely layer the ingredients in the jar as shown at left, making each layer as level as possible without pressing it down.

3. Secure the lid, and decorate as desired. (See page 21.) Attach the instructions for making the shortcakes found below.

Yield:
12 shortcakes

In addition to the contents of the jar, you will need to add the following ingredients:

1 1/2 cups buttermilk

2 eggs

1/2 cup solid shortening, such as Crisco

1 teaspoon vanilla extract

CHOCOLATE SHORTCAKES

Preheat the oven to 350°F. In a large bowl, combine the buttermilk, eggs, shortening, and vanilla extract, and blend with an electric mixer set on low speed for 30 seconds. Add the contents of the jar, and continue to blend for 3 minutes. Pour the batter into a greased 9-x-13-inch baking pan and bake for 25 to 30 minutes, or until a toothpick inserted in the center of the cake comes out clean. Cool completely in the pan before cutting into 12 squares and topping with strawberries and whipped cream. Serve immediately, or store in an airtight container for up to 1 week.

JarCakes

APPLESAUCEJARCAKE

Fragrant with apple and spices, these handy jar cakes
won't remain in your pantry for long!

2²/₃ cups sugar

2 cups applesauce

4 eggs

²/₃ cup solid
shortening, such as
Crisco

²/₃ cup water

3¹/₃ cups all-purpose
flour

2 teaspoons
baking soda

¹/₂ teaspoon
baking powder

I teaspoon salt

I teaspoon cinnamon

I teaspoon
ground cloves

1. Preheat the oven to 325°F. Generously coat 8 pint-size wide-mouth canning jars with cooking spray, and set aside.

2. Place the sugar, applesauce, eggs, shortening, and water in a large mixing bowl, and blend with an electric mixer set on high speed for 2 minutes.

3. Add the flour, baking soda, baking powder, salt, cinnamon, and cloves, and blend on medium speed for 2 additional minutes.

4. Spoon 1 level cup of batter into each jar, and carefully wipe the rims clean of any batter. Arrange the jars on a cookie sheet, and place in the center of the oven.

5. Bake uncovered for 35 to 40 minutes, or until a toothpick inserted in the center of a jar cake comes out clean. Do not underbake.

6. As soon as the jars come out of the oven, carefully put each lid and ring in place, and screw the tops tightly shut. *Be sure to use potholders to screw the lids on as the jars will be hot!*

7. Transfer the jars to wire racks and allow to cool completely. The jar cakes will seal as they cool, making a pinging sound as the vacuum forms.

8. Insure that each jar has sealed properly by using one of the techniques explained on page 15. An unsealed jar cake should be stored in the refrigerator and consumed within a few days. A properly sealed jar may be stored in the pantry for up to 4 months. If giving the jar as a gift, decorate as desired (see page 21) and attach the tag found below.

APPLESAUCE JAR CAKE

Your Applesauce Jar Cake was actually baked *in the Mason jar.*
For best results, be sure to serve your cake within a week.
Simply open the jar and run a butter knife around the cake to
loosen it. Then tip the jar, allowing the cake to slide out.
Enjoy!

CHOCOLATELOVER'SJARCAKE

Keep this cake on hand and you'll never have to leave the house to
satisfy a craving for chocolate. Just open the jar for instant satisfaction!

YIELD:
6 PINT-SIZED
JAR CAKES
(2 SERVINGS EACH)

2 cups all-purpose
flour

2 cups sugar

1 cup butter

1 cup water

¼ cup cocoa powder

½ cup buttermilk

2 eggs

1 teaspoon
vanilla extract

1 teaspoon
baking soda

1. Preheat the oven to 325°F. Generously coat 6 pint-size wide-mouth canning jars with cooking spray, and set aside.

2. In a large mixing bowl, combine the flour and sugar. Set aside.

3. Place the butter, water, and cocoa powder in a small saucepan, and quickly bring to a boil over medium-high heat.

4. Remove the butter mixture from the heat and pour it over the flour mixture. Mix well.

5. Add the buttermilk, eggs, vanilla extract, and baking soda to the batter, and mix well.

6. Spoon 1 level cup of batter into each jar, and carefully wipe the rims clean of any batter. Arrange the jars on a cookie sheet, and place in the center of the oven.

7. Bake uncovered for 35 to 40 minutes, or until a toothpick inserted in the center of a jar cake comes out clean. Do not underbake.

8. As soon as the jars come out of the oven, carefully put each lid and ring in place, and screw the tops tightly shut. *Be sure to use potholders to screw the lids on as the jars will be hot!*

9. Transfer the jars to wire racks and allow to cool completely. The jar cakes will seal as they cool, making a pinging sound as the vacuum forms.

10. Insure that each jar has sealed properly by using one of the techniques explained on page 15. An unsealed jar cake should be stored in the refrigerator and consumed within a few days. A properly sealed jar may be stored in the pantry for up to 4 months. If giving the jar as a gift, decorate as desired (see page 21) and attach the tag found below.

Chocolate Lover's Jar Cake

Your Chocolate Lover's Jar Cake was actually baked *in the Mason jar.* For best results, be sure to serve your cake within a week. Simply open the jar and run a butter knife around the cake to loosen it. Then tip the jar, allowing the cake to slide out. Enjoy!

NUTTYCARAMELJARCAKE

Caramel cake is a favorite in the South. If you've never tried one, now is the time to indulge in this sinfully sweet dessert.

YIELD:
6 PINT-SIZED
JAR CAKES
(2 SERVINGS EACH)

2 cups brown sugar, packed

²/₃ cup sugar

I cup butter, softened

4 eggs

²/₃ cup milk

2 teaspoons vanilla extract

3¹/₂ cups all-purpose flour

2 teaspoons baking soda

I teaspoon baking powder

I teaspoon salt

I cup chopped walnuts

1. Preheat the oven to 325°F. Generously coat 6 pint-size wide-mouth canning jars with cooking spray, and set aside.

2. Place the brown sugar, sugar, butter, eggs, milk, and vanilla extract in a large mixing bowl, and blend with an electric mixer set on high speed for 2 minutes.

3. Add the flour, baking soda, baking powder, and salt, and blend on medium speed for 2 additional minutes. Using a wooden spoon or spatula, stir in the walnuts.

4. Spoon 1 level cup of batter into each jar, and carefully wipe the rims clean of any batter. Arrange the jars on a cookie sheet, and place in the center of the oven.

5. Bake uncovered for 45 to 50 minutes or until a toothpick inserted in the center of a jar cake comes out clean. Do not underbake.

6. As soon as the jars come out of the oven, carefully put each lid and ring in place, and screw the tops tightly shut. *Be sure to use potholders to screw the lids on as the jars will be hot!*

7. Transfer the jars to wire racks and allow to cool completely. The jar cakes will seal as they cool, making a pinging sound as the vacuum forms.

8. Insure that each jar has sealed properly by using one of the techniques explained on page 15. An unsealed jar cake should be stored in the refrigerator and consumed within a few days. A properly sealed jar may be stored in the pantry for up to 4 months. If giving the jar as a gift, decorate as desired (see page 21) and attach the tag found below.

Nutty Caramel Jar Cake

Your Nutty Caramel Jar Cake was actually baked *in the Mason jar.* For best results, be sure to serve your cake within a week. Simply open the jar and run a butter knife around the cake to loosen it. Then tip the jar, allowing the cake to slide out.
Enjoy!

PINACOLADAJARCAKE

With all the flavors of a tropical drink,
this cake is a wonderful choice for a mid-summer dessert.

YIELD:
8 PINT-SIZED
JAR CAKES
(2 SERVINGS EACH)

3 1/2 cups light brown
sugar, packed

3/4 cup butter

4 eggs

1 1/2 cups drained
unsweetened crushed
pineapple, puréed in
blender

1/2 cup dark rum

3 1/3 cups all-purpose
flour

1 1/2 teaspoons
baking powder

1 teaspoon
baking soda

1 cup sweetened
flaked coconut

1. Preheat the oven to 325°F. Generously coat 8 pint-size wide-mouth canning jars with cooking spray, and set aside.

2. Place the brown sugar, butter, and eggs in a large mixing bowl, and blend with an electric mixer set on high speed for 2 minutes.

3. Add the pineapple purée and the rum, and blend on medium speed until well combined.

4. Add the flour, baking powder, and baking soda, and blend on medium speed for 2 additional minutes. Using a wooden spoon or spatula, stir in the coconut.

5. Spoon 1 level cup of batter into each jar, and carefully wipe the rims clean of any batter. Arrange the jars on a cookie sheet, and place in the center of the oven.

6. Bake uncovered for 35 to 40 minutes, or until a toothpick inserted in the center of a jar cake comes out clean. Do not underbake.

7. As soon as the jars come out of the oven, carefully put each lid and ring in place, and screw the tops tightly shut. *Be sure to use potholders to screw the lids on as the jars will be hot!*

8. Transfer the jars to wire racks and allow to cool completely. The jar cakes will seal as they cool, making a pinging sound as the vacuum forms.

9. Insure that each jar has sealed properly by using one of the techniques explained on page 15. An unsealed jar cake should be stored in the refrigerator and consumed within a few days. A properly sealed jar may be stored in the pantry for up to 4 months. If giving the jar as a gift, decorate as desired (see page 21) and attach the tag found below.

PIÑA COLADA JAR CAKE

Your Piña Colada Jar Cake was actually baked *in the Mason jar*.
For best results, be sure to serve your cake within a week.
Simply open the jar and run a butter knife around the cake to
loosen it. Then tip the jar, allowing the cake to slide out.
Enjoy!

PUMPKINSPICEJARCAKE

Moist and aromatic with cinnamon, ginger, and cloves,
this is the perfect dessert for the spice cake lover in your house.

YIELD:
**8 PINT-SIZED
JAR CAKES
(2 SERVINGS EACH)**

3 1/2 cups light brown
sugar, packed

2 cups canned
pumpkin

4 eggs

3/4 cup butter,
softened

3 1/3 cups all-purpose
flour

1 1/2 teaspoons
baking powder

1 teaspoon
baking soda

1 teaspoon cinnamon

1/2 teaspoon ginger

1/4 teaspoon
ground cloves

1 cup chopped
walnuts

1. Preheat the oven to 325°F. Generously coat 8 pint-size wide-mouth canning jars with cooking spray, and set aside.

2. Place the brown sugar, pumpkin, eggs, and butter in a large mixing bowl, and blend with an electric mixer set on high speed for 2 minutes.

3. Add the flour, baking powder, baking soda, cinnamon, ginger, and cloves, and blend on medium speed for 2 additional minutes. Using a wooden spoon or spatula, stir in the walnuts.

4. Spoon 1 level cup of batter into each jar, and carefully wipe the rims clean of any batter. Arrange the jars on a cookie sheet, and place in the center of the oven.

5. Bake uncovered for 35 to 40 minutes, or until a toothpick inserted in the center of a jar cake comes out clean. Do not underbake.

6. As soon as the jars come out of the oven, carefully put each lid and ring in place, and screw the tops tightly shut. *Be sure to use potholders to screw the lids on as the jars will be hot!*

7. Transfer the jars to wire racks and allow to cool completely. The jar cakes will seal as they cool, making a pinging sound as the vacuum forms.

8. Insure that each jar has sealed properly by using one of the techniques explained on page 15. An unsealed jar cake should be stored in the refrigerator and consumed within a few days. A properly sealed jar may be stored in the pantry for up to 4 months. If giving the jar as a gift, decorate as desired (see page 21) and attach the tag found below.

PUMPKIN SPICE JAR CAKE

Your Pumpkin Spice Jar Cake was actually baked *in the Mason jar*. For best results, be sure to serve your cake within a week. Simply open the jar and run a butter knife around the cake to loosen it. Then tip the jar, allowing the cake to slide out. Enjoy!

Metric Conversion Tables

Common Liquid Conversions

Measurement	=	Milliliters
$1/4$ teaspoon	=	1.25 milliliters
$1/2$ teaspoon	=	2.50 milliliters
$3/4$ teaspoon	=	3.75 milliliters
1 teaspoon	=	5.00 milliliters
$1 1/4$ teaspoons	=	6.25 milliliters
$1 1/2$ teaspoons	=	7.50 milliliters
$1 3/4$ teaspoons	=	8.75 milliliters
2 teaspoons	=	10.0 milliliters
1 tablespoon	=	15.0 milliliters
2 tablespoons	=	30.0 milliliters

Measurement	=	Liters
$1/4$ cup	=	0.06 liters
$1/2$ cup	=	0.12 liters
$3/4$ cup	=	0.18 liters
1 cup	=	0.24 liters
$1 1/4$ cups	=	0.30 liters
$1 1/2$ cups	=	0.36 liters
2 cups	=	0.48 liters
$2 1/2$ cups	=	0.60 liters
3 cups	=	0.72 liters
$3 1/2$ cups	=	0.84 liters
4 cups	=	0.96 liters
$4 1/2$ cups	=	1.08 liters
5 cups	=	1.20 liters
$5 1/2$ cups	=	1.32 liters

Conversion Formulas

LIQUID		
When You Know	Multiply By	To Determine
teaspoons	5.0	milliliters
tablespoons	15.0	milliliters
fluid ounces	30.0	milliliters
cups	0.24	liters
pints	0.47	liters
quarts	0.95	liters

WEIGHT		
When You Know	Multiply By	To Determine
ounces	28.0	grams
pounds	0.45	kilograms

Converting Fahrenheit to Celsius

Fahrenheit	=	Celsius
200–205	=	95
220–225	=	105
245–250	=	120
275	=	135
300–305	=	150
325–330	=	165
345–350	=	175
370–375	=	190
400–405	=	205
425–430	=	220
445–450	=	230
470–475	=	245
500	=	260

Index

THE MASON JAR COOKIE COOKBOOK
How to Create Mason Jar Cookie Mixes
Lonnette Parks

Nothing gladdens the heart like the tantalizing aroma of cookies baking in the oven. But for so many people, a busy lifestyle has made it impossible to find the time to bake at home—until now. Lonnette Parks, cookie baker extraordinaire, has not only developed fifty kitchen-tested recipes for delicious cookies, but has found a way for you to give the gift of home baking to everyone on your gift list.

For each mouth-watering cookie, the author provides the full recipe so that you can bake a variety of delights at home. In addition, she presents complete instructions for beautifully arranging the nonperishable ingredients in a Mason jar so that you can give the jar to a friend. By adding just a few common ingredients, your friend can then prepare fabulous home-baked cookies in a matter of minutes. Recipes include Best Ever Chocolate Chip Cookies, Blondies, and much, much more.

Whether you want to bake scrumptious cookies in your own kitchen or you'd like to give distinctive Mason jar cookie mixes to cookie-loving friends and family, *The Mason Jar Cookie Cookbook* is the perfect book.

$12.95 US / $21.00 CAN • 144 pages • 7.5 x 7.5-inch quality paperback • 2-Color • ISBN 0-7570-0046-0

THE MASON JAR SOUP-TO-NUTS COOKBOOK
How to Create Mason Jar Recipe Mixes
Lonnette Parks

In this follow-up to her best-selling book, *The Mason Jar Cookie Cookbook,* author and cook Lonnette Parks presents recipes for over fifty delicious soups, muffins, breads, cakes, pancakes, beverages, and more. And, just as in her previous book, the author tells you how to give the gift of home cooking to friends and family.

For each Mason jar creation, the author provides the full recipe so that you can cook and bake a variety of delights at home. In addition, she includes complete instructions for beautifully arranging the nonperishable ingredients in a Mason jar so that you can give the jar to a friend. Recipes include Golden Corn Bread, Double Chocolate Biscotti, Ginger Muffins, Apple Cinnamon Pancakes, Barley Rice Soup, Viennese Coffee, and much, much more.

$12.95 US / $21.00 CAN • 144 pages • 7.5 x 7.5-inch quality paperback • 2-Color • ISBN 0-7570-0129-7

MRS. CUBBISON'S BEST STUFFING COOKBOOK
Sensational Stuffings for Poultry, Meats, Fish, Side Dishes, and More
Edited by Leo Pearlstein and Lisa Messinger

When you think of stuffing, you probably picture Thanksgiving, turkey, and traditional dinner fare. But now that people all over the country are enjoying exciting new flavors, from fusion cooking to ethnic cuisine, maybe it's time to add a little pizzazz to your stuffing—and to your everyday meals, as well! Designed to take stuffing to new culinary heights, here is a superb collection of creative recipes from America's number-one stuffing expert, Mrs. Sophie Cubbison.

Mrs. Cubbison's Best Stuffing Cookbook is a complete guide to the art of making delicious stuffing. It begins with the basics of preparing stuffing, and then offers one hundred easy-to-make kitchen-tested recipes—from Jambalaya Stuffing to Asian Ginger Stir-Fried, and from Citrus Yam Stuffing to Onion Soufflé. Within its "Shaping Up" chapter, you'll learn how to turn stuffing into mouth-watering muffins, pick-up appetizers, and tempting desserts. Mrs. Cubbison has even included delicious low-fat, reduced-calorie recipes! With *Mrs. Cubbison's Best Stuffing Cookbook* in hand, you can add a touch of creativity not only to your holiday celebrations, but to every meal that you and your family enjoy.

$14.95 US / $22.50 CAN • 156 Pages • 7.5 x 7.5-inch quality paperback • ISBN 0-7570-0260-9

THE SOURDOUGH BREAD BOWL COOKBOOK
For Parties, Holiday Celebrations, Family Gatherings, and Everyday Meals
John Vrattos and Lisa Messinger

For decades, tens of thousands of visitors to San Francisco's famed Fisherman's Wharf have enjoyed crusty sourdough bread bowls filled with piping hot chowder. As the popularity of this culinary treat grew, so did the many creative uses of Sourdough Bread Bowls—from party centerpieces filled with luscious dips to edible settings for salads, entrées, and more. To answer the question, "How do I get started?" gourmet chef John Vrattos and best-selling food writer Lisa Messinger have created a cookbook that provides all the answers. After presenting easy-to-follow instructions for carving out a bread bowl, they offer dozens of kitchen-tested recipes, ranging from traditional dishes such as San Francisco's famed Clam Chowder to the innovative Warm Baja Shrimp Taco Dip. You'll even find recipes developed by top restaurant chefs.

Whether you're hosting a Superbowl party, having the family over for dinner, or simply cooking up an intimate supper for two, make your event a little more special with *The Sourdough Bread Bowl Cookbook.*

$14.95 US / $22.50 CAN • 156 Pages • 7.5 x 7.5-inch quality paperback • ISBN 0-7570-0149-1

For more information about our books, visit our website at www.squareonepublishers.com